AF539427

NUTRITION EDUCATION

NUTRITION EDUCATION

V. SREEDEVI
Dept. of Home Science
S.V. University
Tirupati - 517502 (A.P.)

DISCOVERY PUBLISHING HOUSE PVT. LTD.
NEW DELHI-110 002

First Published – 1997

Reprinted – 2025

ISBN: 978-81-7141-344-7

Nutrition Eduction

Published by:

DISCOVERY PUBLISHING HOUSE
4383/4B, Ansari Road, Darya Ganj
New Delhi-110 002 (India)
Phone: +91-11-23279245; 23253475; 43596065
Mobile: +91 9811179893 / +91 9871656464
E-mail: discoverybooksindia@gmail.com
orderdphbooks@gmail.com
namitwasan9@gmail.com
web: www.discoverypublishinggroup.com

Printed at:
Infinity Imaging Systems
Delhi

Dedicated to

My

Beloved Parents

Contents

Acknowledgements

I am indebted to express my deep sense of gratitude to my Research Supervisor Prof. V.L.N. Reddy whose diligent supervision, scholarship and wisdom nurtured the growth and defined the direction throughout the course of my research and without which this venture would not have fructified.

I am highly grateful to Dr. B. Niranjan Reddy, Head, Department of Adult Education for his valuable suggestions, constant encouragement during the course of my study.

I feel inadequacy of my diction to express my gratitude to Dr. S. Padmanabaiah, Reader in Education for his priceless guidance offered which moulded and destined the strategy of my investigation.

I am extremely thankful to my friend Mrs. R. Prathyusha and my beloved daughter N. Shalini Reddy for the untiring help rendered by them in coding and tabulation of the data, whcih provided initial momentum and pace to this study.

I am specially thankful to Dr. M. Ubaidullah for his timely help, good co-operaiton and helpful suggestions in furnishing this thesis.

My thanks are due to Dr. C. Subba Rami Reddy, Dr. P. Balasiddamuni, Sri B. Prabhakar Reddy, Sri B. Ramachandra Reddy and Sri D. Ramakrishnaiah for their suggestions regarding statistical analysis. I affectionately reminisce the profound inspiration inculcated in me by my friends Dr. S. Rathna Kumari and Dr. D. Jamuna.

I would like to record my appreciation to Sri R.A. Jayantha for correcting the thesis.

I also thank Prof. N. Munuswamy, who was cooperative in coining computer programmes for data analysis with the computer firm M/s Sri Venkateswara Computer System, Balaji Colony, Tirupati, who analysed the data diligently in required time.

I am thankful to Dr. D. Gunasekhar, Mr. M.V.L. Reddy and Mr. K. Indrasena Reddy for helping in proof reading.

I express my sincere and heartfelt gratitude to all the respondents of the study who cheerfully cooperated and helped me in carrying out the investigation successfully.

My thanks are due to the Project Officers, Assistant Project Officers, Supervisors of the Projects concerned for their cooperation in the collection of data.

Mr. Jayachandra Reddy had applied his drafting talents to the preparation of the abacs. My thanks are due to him.

I wish to place on record the affectionate help and ambitious encouragement rendered by my mother Mrs. V. Subbalakshumamma and brother V.S. Gopinath. I thank them reverentrally.

I am at loss of words to describe the forbearance evinced by my betterhalf Mr. N. Purushotham Reddy who had to bear with the mundane distractions that cropped up due to my busy involvement in research.

Last but not the least, I thank Sri G. Siri Babu for typing the thesis judiciously and expeditiously.

V. Sreedevi

1
Nutrition Education—An Overview

"Improving female education is one of the primary ways of improving the health of children"

(Chandler, 1985)

Introduction

India's food and nutrition problems continue to be formidable and malnutrition is still one of the crucial problems in the process of development. Nearly two-thirds of India's population is on a nutritionally deficient diet. Nutritional surveys conducted and repeated over a number of years have indicated that a majority of population of every age group, including both the sexes, suffer from malnutrition bordering on both calorie and protein starvation and a complete lack of protective foods rich in minerals and vitamins (Gopalan, 1966; Ranganathan, 1968; Devadas, 1972; NIN Annual Reports, 1981; 1982).

Malnutrition affects people in general, but its adverse effects are more pronounced among the vulnerable groups of women and children in rural and urban areas. Several studies support this statement (NNMB Surveys, 1977; ICMR, 1977; Gopalan, 1973; NIN Annual Reports, 1978; 1980; 1981; 1982; ICMR, 1985).

The determinants of malnutrition at different levels are many. At the individual level food, nutrient intake and its utilization depend on factors like age, physiological and pathological status of the person. At the macro level general inadequacy of food, population growth, etc., are operative Overlapping the micro and macro levels, there are socio-economic and cultural factors like purchasing capacity of the family, family size, food habits and beliefs, health aspects and environment, which directly influence the diet of people (Kamala Gopala Rao, 1983).

Malnutrition is not exclusively due to non-availability of nutritious food. Failure to use the available resources in a meaningful manner can be another cause. This is mainly due to lack of knowledge of the value of foods in relation to the needs of the individual. Ignorance and superstition play a great role in the rejection of locally available cheap nutritious foods (Shanthi Chakravarthy, 1977; Raju et al., 1977).

Financial constraints alone cannot be taken as the basis for the prevailing malnutritional status. A majority of the people, no matter of what class, have status symbols, which force them to spend their income for purposes other than that of securing food. Even when more money is spent on food it is spent on the wrong types of foods (Davidson et al., 1973; Raju et al., 1977). Solving the problem of malnutrition therefore involves not only having the food to eat but also the proper selection, preparation and consumption of foods (Shanthi Chakravarthy, 1977). Food behaviour is therefore an important issue in determining the nutritional status.

Nutrition intervention programmes have been taken up and are being implemented by the Central and State Governments and voluntary agencies with a view to ameliorating the nutritional status and health of the vulnerable sections of the population. Obviously any attempt to supplement the diet of this population by external inputs alone is going to be beyond the capacity of the country or any charitable organisation (Devadas, 1977). The improvement of nutritional status of the people cannot be brought about through an adhoc, isolated feeding programme (Gopalan, 1977). The programmes have to promote a sustained behavioural changes.

In this context, we are mindful of the slogan used by the international food agencies, which illustrates the philosophy of Chinese proverb "give a man a fish and feed him for a day; teach a man to fish and you feed him for life time" (Winter, 1970). This may be paraphrased as 'Give a child a meal and you relieve his immediate hunger. Teach his mother to feed him well and this will benefit him for years, it will also help the rest of his family and possibly his neighbour and the wider community" (Cutting, 1975).

The magnitude of malnutrition and the ignorance about the relationship of food to health among a majority of the population project the need for nutrition education at all levels. This approach in the long run may promote self reliance and self support in the communities.

Deliberate and sustained nutrition education has been recognised as a potent weapon for prevention and control of malnutrition. Obviously the goal of these educational efforts ought to be beyond mere transfer of information. What is envisaged is to motivate and bring about behavioural changes among the community members in the choice of foods (Ramadas Murthy, 1982).

Meaning

Nutrition Education is the foundation for any programme intended for nutritional improvement (Devadas et al 1970).

Albanese (1971) defines nutrition education as a means of translating nutritional requirements into food and adjusting the food choices to satisfy nutritional, cultural, psychological and economic needs.

The American Dietetic Association (1973) defined nutritional education as the process by which beliefs, attitudes, environmental influences and understandings about food leads to practices that are scientifically sound, practical, and consistent with individual needs and available food resources. Leverton (1974) stated that it is a multidisciplinary process that involves the transfer of information, development of motivation and modification of food habits where needed.

According to Obert (1978), it is the process of applying knowledge of nutrition related scientific information of social and behavioural sciences in ways designed to influence individuals and groups to cat the kinds and amount of foods that will make a maximum contribution to health and social satisfaction. The importance of nutrition education was stressed by White (1976) who stated that for making judicious food choices and for the achievement of one's genetic potential, the knowledge of nutrition is imperative.

All the above definitions suggest that nutrition education aims at bringing in nutrition behaviours which promote health of an individual.

Need

The nutritional profile of the Indian women and children focus on the need to take active steps towards prevention of malnutrition. Behar (1977), the chief of the nutrition unit of W.H.O. stated that malnutrition is a man made problem and he further emphasized that ignorance is, in many instances, the most important cause of malnutrition, particularly in the case of small children whose mothers do not know how to feed them properly. William (1969), Robinson (1972) and Nagwekar (1972) made similar observations and stressed the need to overcome 'ignorance' through educating mothers in nutrition.

The Indian Paediatrician, Ghosh (1977) reported that the ignorance of parents about the requirements of children is the most important cause of malnutrition in India and particularly when the child is dependent on his mother for food. The Indian mother cannot believe that her 1 to 2 year old child needs roughly half the food which she herself eats. The mother of the pre-school child usually has the primary responsibility for introducing the child to new foods for helping the child to develop food habits. The foods the mother makes available in the home, and the mothers' use of the food are influenced by her beliefs, attitudes, knowledge of food and nutrition (Eppright et al 1970; Lowenberg, et al 1970). Therefore, the women's role in improving the nutritional status of their families is particularly important, for they are the family caterers (Greaves, 1975).

Many investigators (Manocha, 1972; Shah, 1978; Ghosh, 1977; Jelliffe, 1968) reported that malnutrition set in due to late introduction of solids to the infants, less number of feeds and unhygienic food provided for children. These observations suggest that mothers' awareness about proper feeding practices is essential for improving the nutritional status of their children.

Principles

Jelliffe (1968) stated that education which is geared to improve the local conditions and is based on local needs and freed from the local cultural beliefs is most likely to be successful. He stressed that the most single aim to nutrition education is to persuade mothers in the tropics to make the best use of foods locally available for feeding children in the early years of life.

Williams (1974) stated that the beliefs and practices of people have psychological and sociological functions, and that change of customs should be brought about by way of persuasion and demonstration and not by hostile methods. He expressed that each person has culturally determined systems of values and that any attempt to impart nutritional knowledge by force is unlikely to meet with success. He suggested active involvement of people in group discussions in order to create awareness of their needs and to motivate them for action. He furter emphasized that evaluation of different methods for behavioural change are of practical importance.

Stanfield (1976) discussed several principles of nutrition education. They are identification, involvement, indigenous, influencers, indoctrination, integration and individuals. Nutrition education should appear relevant to the target population who should be to identify with it. Participants should be as actively involved as possible. Indigenous means of communication such as proverbs, songs, dances, drama and pictures should be used. Influential persons should be involved and used as role models. Nutrition education should concentrate on a few simple themes which are emphasized repeatedly. Food intake can be influenced by a large number of factors, all of these should be considered. Initiative, imagination, innovation and interest are desirable qualities of the individual teacher in any successful education programme. Evaluation is important for three main reasons; to confirm or modify the methodology, to motivate the staff, to convince the authorities of the usefulness of the programme.

Munoz De Chavez (1972) stated that even though the task of improving dietary habits in a community is difficult there are also factors conducive to change. The educator must be aware of both situations to take advantage to them and use them in his/her methodology. Drastic changes are to be avoided. Minor changes have the advantage of being possible even where the socio economic status of a community living at a subsistence level cannot be altered.

Ritchie (1969) suggested that in a nutrition education programme advice must be practicable, the changes suggested minimal, and acceptable. The researcher also emphasized the importance of suggesting a change after seeking satisfactory substitute and to base education on the foods used and practices followed by people.

Approaches

The educational process involves the use of all the methods, techniques, procedures and illustrative materials to influence individual food practices.

In the Indian context methods used with illiterate people include demonstrations, dramatizations and songs, films, discussions, meetings, exhibitions, field trips, gardening activities and cooking competitions. These methods are described and compared as to their effectiveness by Devadas and Usha Chandrasekhar (1970). The investigators visited 50 families and elicited the information by asking questions. The ability of the mothers to repeat the theme of the education programme formed the basis of rating. Those which were mentioned with minimal reminder were rated as effective. When no mention was made, it was categorized as least effective. Results indicated that demonstration was the best method for the adult audience. Dramatizations and songs taught to children impress their minds and prompt them to act accordingly. Exhibitions when explained well, could serve as good medium for nutrition education. The authors stated that interventions can only succeed if they take account of economic and social conditions as well as cultural patterns of the people concerned. Only multifaceted approaches through different channels, repetition and living examples can bring about desirable changes permanently.

Carruth et al (1971) conducted a study to find out the increase and retention of knowledge by cartoon approach in nutrition education. The experimental groups' knowledge improved after the exposure to nutrition education. The retention test scores revealed that the amount of information lost during six weeks time lapse was not statistically significant.

Manoff (1980) reported the efforts made in giving nutrition education through mass media. Mass media programmes changed food habits and beliefs with respect to infant feeding and child care in Ecuador, Nicaragua and the Phillippines. In order to succeed the messages must respond to needs of the target population and above all, they must reach that population. Radio messages, calenders, posters, pamphlets/note books and comic books were used in a nutrition education campaign in Korea (Higgins et al., 1972). The main message was that a balanced diet should contain foods from each of five food groups. The programme evaluators felt that radio messages were too varied and sophisticated. Posters were not as well received as calenders. The most receptive audience was young and educated and middle class. City dwellers seemed to be more receptive than local population. Older age groups and people at the lowest economic and educational level were less affected by the campaign.

Guthrie (1981) reported about the three different approaches used to motivate women to learn to continue breast feeding, supplement breast milk with other food, plant green leafy vegetables, obtain weight gain, visit health centre once a month. Mothers in 3 villages in Phillippines were encouraged to follow the above five rules. Mothers in the first village received health coupons which could be traded in for food, soap or clothing. In the second village the mothers received the colour photograph of themselves and their baby, if the baby maintained his weight for age status for three months. In the third village no reward system was offered, but nutrition education and medical service were offered. Both reward systems worked equally well.

Swarnalatha (1978) conducted a study on the relative effectiveness of four teaching approaches using behaviour modification, functional, consistency and information processing approaches in four villages. Rural mothers having children 0 to 11 years of age formed the study group. Education about the diet of children was imparted to them. Flash cards were used as medium of teaching. The results showed that functional and behavioural modification were superior to the remaining approaches. Consistency approach was the least effective approach. A similar study was carried out by Amala Kumari (1979) in imparting nutrition education to urban mothers. She found that functional and behaviour modification approaches were superior to the other approaches studied.

A study on comparison of mass media techniques and direct method for nutrition education in rural Mexico was conducted by Cerqueira et al (1979). The objective of this study was to determine the effectiveness of mass media techniques compared to direct, traditional methods of education in transmitting the basic concepts of hygiene, health and nutrition. Three comparable rural communities were selected in the state of Mexico, their test populations became the mass media, direct education and control groups. Available food resources, dietary habits and nutrition related knowledge was assessed by questionnaire immediately after the programme, three months later and one year later. The results obtained by the two methods were both encouraging and did not differ significantly. The control group which also received radio messages responded negatively by increasing their consumption of foods of low nutritive value.

The results of these investigations indicate that selection of message and method are crucial to the success of any nutrition education programme. The target group reached also differed in various contexts. In the Western context, it is a highly educated groups whereas, in the East Asian context, it is either an illiterative or very low literate group. The contrasting situations limit the scope of generalisation of results. Thus, there is a need to investigate the influence of factors such as the need, nature of group and other demographic characteristics of the target group on the impact of nutrition education programmes.

Factors Influencing Nutrition Related Behaviour

The nutritonal status of an individual is the final outcome of many interacting factors operating simultaneously and concurrently on the individual in the physical, ecological and cultural setting of the community. The food habits and practices reflect the cultural, social and educational values and the economic conditions of a community. They are the outcomes of the sum total of numerous influences–thoughts, sentiments, beliefs and activities in a group or community. Food habits indicate not only the practices in selecting, combining, cooking and eating food but also the psychological, social and emotional values of food.

Nearly 70 per cent of India's population live in the rural areas. They are bound together by time-honoured customs, traditions, rights and taboos which govern their communities. Eventually distinctive food preferences and prejudices are formed. A few of the factors influencing the nutrition related behaviours are considered here. Parvathi Rao (1968) stated some of the social and cultural factors that influence the nutritional behaviour.

Status of the Members of the Society and Family Cohesiveness

Food distribution depends upon the status, role and interpersonal relationship among the members of the family rather than on their nutritional needs. The senior and earning male members or the wage earners are served first and are given the best diet both in quantity and quality while the vulnerable segments namely children and women of child bearing age get the left overs.

Influence of Head or Other Members in the Family

The head of the family influences the dietary pattern directly by making all the purchases himself or indirectly by making his tastes known so that the women of the home are forced to cook foods of his choice. In the matters of child feeding and the diets of pregnant and lactating mothers, mother-in-law and grandmothers often have an authority.

Value Systems

Parvathi Rao (1968) found in her survey that even among so called better off families, it is the quantity and not the quality of the food that increases with wealth. Surveys have revealed that expenditure on gold, festivals and funerals ranged between 50 to 150 per cent of the total income. In addition to the above, Devadas (1968, 1974) presented the following factors as those influencing the nutrition behaviour of people.

Income (Poverty)

Poverty is caused by numerous social, economic and individual components. Income decides the standard of living of a family. Several surveys conducted in rural areas reveal that nearly 80 per cent is spent on food. Of the food expenditure, cereals claim nearly 60 per cent and above, the rest is distributed for the other foods. As a result the diets consumed are inadequate in protective foods. On the other hand, there are population groups who are well to do but due to lack of knowledge suffer from nutritional deficiencies.

Family Size

The children from small families had lesser evidence of nutritional deficiencies than children from large families.

Customs, Beliefs, Traditions and Attitudes

Prevailing customs may prevent people from consuming valuable food, even when they are available. Beliefs are crucial in the acceptance or rejection of foods. Tastes and practices governed by traditions make people sacrifice economic gain for something as esteemed as quality.

Prestige and Caste Status Symbols

Foods are an expression of wealth, prestige and social status in all cultures. Prestige demands that on should have rare and costly varieties of food. Tne foods that are grown in abundance and available at free of cost, such as green leafy vegetables and foods which are less expensive such as papaya and amla are regarded as disdain. Prestige may also be a stimulant to changes in food habits.

Ignorance

Ignorance is perhaps the most important single factor influencing the nutritional practices in the Indian context and with special reference to rural areas (Devadas, 1974; Parvathi Rao, 1968). One important well accepted finding in nutrition is that malnutrition is related to poverty, ignorance and indifference (While, 1976).

The urban slum dwellers and the poor sections of the rural areas are not even aware that they are sick because they do not know what it is to be well (Manocha, 1972). Berg (1973) pointed that an important part of nutrition gap is information gap. Achaya (1974) has commented that in many Indian communities the importance of a special weaning food for children is not realised and hence education of the mothers in this regard would be very necessary to increase the demand for such a food.

Education

Illiteracy is the greatest barrier to any improvement in the position of women. Approximately 50 (49.2) per cent of women in the age group 15–35 years are illiterate. While the literacy rate has slowly improved, the actual number of illiterates has been increasing due to the rising population and the backlog of adult illiteracy. More so in the case of women. The literacy for females has consistently been behind that for males, and that too by a big margin. The female literacy rate in rural India, where three-fourths of the people live, has been around a third of the female literacy rate for the towns (Census of India, 1981).

The correlation between female illiteracy and infant mortality is equally clear. It is found that infant mortality was highest in the case of illiterate mothers both in urban and rural areas but much higher in the latter (Survey of Infant and Child Mortality, 1979). The lack of education of women limits their awareness of the benefits of learning for their children.

The national aim is to reach by 1995 all adults in the age group of 15–35 through non-formal and formal channels of education. There are about 115.7 million illiterate women. Of this only about five million are being presently reached through various adult education programmes including functional literacy schemes for women. Motivating adult learners is listed as one of the challenges to be met.

Though various factors are listed as influencing the nutrition related behaviours, there is very limited knowledge to thoroughly explain the role of these in different contexts. The family's life style is the result of many interacting factors and there is a need to study these to understand the behaviours related to nutrition.

Behavioural Changes Related to Nutrition Education

Nutritional well being of a population depends on the interaction of a multitude of socio-economic and cultural factors. A wide range of variables in the production, processing and consumer systems, if properly analysed in an integrated way, may explain the nutrition system as well as help in identifying sensitive variables for intervention points. Nutrition education is likely to influence some of the variables directly and some others indirectly. In order to explain the role of nutrition education it is necessary to define it, in terms of some definite parameters. From the nutritionists point of view, a set of information and its awareness, knowledge and perhaps the extent to which this information and knowledge are put to use are of great value (Rajagopalan, 1977).

Assessment of any nutrition education programme must be viewed against the backdrop of existing consumer behaviour, their beliefs and habits.

Education is the process of bringing in desirable changes in human behaviour in knowledge, attitudes and skills, either in all, or one or more of them (Adivi Reddy, 1976). He also explained three kinds of behavioural changes viz., cognitive, affective and psychomotor changes.

Cognitive Change : This includes intellectual outcomes such as knowledge, understanding and thinking skills.

Affective Change : It includes those outcomes that emphasize feeling and emotion such as interests, attitudes, appreciation and methods of adjustment.

Psychomotor Change : It emphasises the motor skills, such as house keeping, sewing, cooking. Usually psychomotor outcomes include both psychological and physical activity. So, cognitive and affective behaviour in turn influence the psychomotor outcomes or psychomotor behaviour.

Various types of nutrition education programmes have been designed and implemented thus exposing many individuals to the principles of sound nutrition. Although specific objectives and goals differ all nutrition education programmes are aimed at a positive change in knowledge, attitude and practices with regard to food and nutrition (Dastur et al., 1977; Devadas et al., 1977; 1979; 1980).

Briggs (1969) stated there is sufficient knowledge on which to base sound nutrition education programme but, much research is still needed to achieve greater success. Devadas (1979) stressed the importance of research in nutrition education in the Indian context, as in many instances poverty, unemployment, ignorance and illiteracy of people make them resistant to changes. The status of women in the society is crucial for the welfare of children and for development. There is a need to raise their status through education programmes apart from other programmes for development.

Gillespe (1981) referred the many constraints encountered in nutrition education indicated by Yarbrough. Changing behaviour is a slow process, people resist changes related to food practices. This is mainly because, advantages of good nutrition are not usually very visible, especially in short terms. Rate of adoption may be slow as food behaviour requires group discussion as well as individual decisions at family level. Given these constraints success in nutrition education should be more surprising than failures. Gillespe stressed that current knowledge is still insufficient to increase greatly the impact of nutrition education.

Many of the nutrition education programmes conducted in the Indian context are based on the needs of the community as identified by the programme implementators, rather than as envisaged by the community members. Non-involvement of the community in the planning and implementation of the programmes, lack of baseline information about the community and their felt needs, have been identified as constraints of nutrition education programmes (Ramadas Murthy, 1982). It has been found that spontaneous change in a community is possible when people themselves identify their felt needs and must want to change (Mead, 1962).

Mead (1962) stated that food habits are not always more difficult to change than other habits. She was of the opinion that strong resistance is only in some people and in some cultures. This view suggests that communities may differ in their adoption of food related behaviours. Information on the impact of nutrition education programmes on various communities which differ in their socio-economic and cultural backgrounds would be of great value in improving the strategies in nutrition education.

Adult Education Programme in India and in Andhra Pradesh

On the front of literacy and adult education in India adequate progress has not been made. The magnitude of illiteracy has been and is colossal to describe in one word and it continues to be so even after the initiation of developmental planning in the country. The effective rates of illiteracy have been decreasing in the country since 1951 but the population of illiterates in the age-group beyond 4 years has been increasing. This is a paradoxical situation. The percentages of illiteracy (excluding the 0–4 age group) in 1951, 1961, 1971, and 1981 were 81.7, 71.7, 65.5 and 58.27 respectively. This trend of decrease of illiteracy is illusory, for the number of people illiterates during the period has been increasing. The absolute number of illiterates in 1951, 1961, 1971 and 1981 was 246.63, 267.22. 307.19 and 343.26 millions respectively.

There are many reasons for this trend of affairs to prevail on the literacy front. Firstly, the allocations made for adult education right upto 1978 have been rather very meagre. Secondly, there was no country-wide programme of adult education until the National Adult Education Programme was launched in 1978 in the country. Thirdly, the programme of adult education in the past have been largely traditional literacy programme which did not motivate the illiterate adults for adult education.

The half-hearted attempts made to spread literacy and adult education may be summarized in the following lines. In 1922 night schools and literacy classes were started in the country. A new schools and colleges and a few provincial governments responded to this call. But this did not gain momentum. Literacy assumed importance in 1937 after the installation of Congress Ministries in the provinces in India. During this period the first mass literacy drive was launched in Bihar and thus it spread to other provinces. But unfortunately after the resignation of the Congress Government in 1939, this movement came to an abrupt end. The weakness of this effort was that it tended to rely excessively on mere literacy, without well planned follow-up activities.

The social education programme that was launched soon after Independence became a part and parcel of the National Extension Service and Community Development. The elements of this programme were : (1) literacy, (2) extension, (3) general education, (4) leadership training, and (5) social consciousness. From the Second Five Year Plan itself the financial provisions for social education began to dwindle and before the end of the Third Plan the pains taken by created structures of social education withered away.

Another programme started in India was the Grama Shakshan Mohim in the Post-Independence Era (1959). The programme was chiefly confined to Maharashtra and the people relapsed into illiteracy after attaining literacy in this programme were many.

The Farmers' Functional Literacy Programme was started in India during 1967-68. The programme covered 150 districts at its peak stage of organisation in 1976. This programme was operated exclusively for farmers and it had to be wounded up when the NAEP was started in 1978.

The National Adult Education Programme, popularly called as NAEP was launched on October 2, 1978 to impart literacy, functionality and awareness to about 100 million people in the age-group of 15–35 years within a period of 5 years from the date of launching of the programme. There was national consensus behind the starting of this programme. This programme made considerable progress ever since it was started. The target period of covering the 100 million illiterates is extended to 1995 subsequently. The programme is operated through Rural Functional Literacy Projects, State Adult Education Projects, Nehru Yuvak Kendras and Non-formal Education and Functional Literacy Projects for Women. Many voluntary organisations are also participating in the programme apart from universities. A few Ministries (Central Ministry of Education and Central Ministry of Labour) are also running adult education centres. To provide technical support, state Resource Centres and one National Resource Centre for non-formal education have been created. At the national level, there is a National Board of Adult Education for formulating policy and issuing guidelines for planning and obtaining coordination. The states have also been advised to set up State Boards of Adult Education for coordinated planning and implementation at the State level.

The National Adult Education Programme was started on October 2, 1979 in Andhra Pradesh. A Directorate of Adult Education, Government of Andhra Pradesh is in-charge of the National Adult Education Programme in the State. The Directorate looks after planning, administration and organisational aspects of the programmes. For every district, there is one Deputy Director to look after the adult education programme in the district. At the project level, the activities of the programme are looked after by the project officer. Supervisors and instructors are under the direct control of project officers.

The NAEP is launched specially for the 15–35 year age-group illiterates. This is a very high fecund group that constitute the population in our country and also it exerts a lot of influence on other walks of life.

The policy statement on adult education notes that there is need to organise special programmes of education to women and to the Scheduled Caste and Scheduled Tribes. The areas of major concern for women are recognised as maternal and child health, nutrition, family relations, women emancipation, etc. High birth rate, high death rate, malnutrition, under-nutrition, higher proness to deficiency diseases and low acceptance of family planning are more prevalent in our country. Hence, there is a great need of food and nutrition education for the adult education programme functionaries and also participants. Nutrition education will help them to overcome some of these problems rapidly. Hence, nutrition education has a rightful place in the education for these groups. The success of the nutrition education programme to a great extent is dependent on the felt needs of the individuals/groups themselves. It is in this context that the present investigation was conceived.

2
Review of Related Literature

Need for Research in Nutrition Education

The need for research in nutrition education arises due to two important factors : (1) Necessity to educate people as to how to use the available foods efficiently, and (2) the evolving nature of the science of nutrition. Further, the extent of hunger and malnutrition both in affluent as well as developing countries suggest that methodology adopted for nutrition education till now has had little effect on food behaviour and nutritional status of the people. Changes taking place in the food behaviour seem to be temporary but not permanent in nature. This condition continues to exist till today. However nutritional status has been improved in select populations of the world where nutrition education was accompanied by food supplementation. Hence, there is a need to evolve effective approaches relevant to the developing population of the world to improve food behaviour.

Davey and Mc Naughton (1969) stated that nutrition education in developing countries had been disappointing. They also indicated that nutrition education programmes bring about changes in three stages (1) understanding, (2) acceptance and (3) practising relating to nutrition. However, no research data were provided by the authors in support of these observations. Until reliable data related to developmental stages of adoption suggested are available, there is little evidence from which one can draw conclusions. Yet, the above statement does not negate the value of nutrition educators' experience and observations.

The few studies on nutrition education as compiled and reviewed by Brun (1985) are enumerated in Table 2.1. Though the studies began in early twentieth century, most of them were conducted during the past 20 years. The more recent studies which were complex in nature have brought out more findings than those studies carried out in previous decades.

Table 2.1 : A Compilation of Nutrition Education Studies during the Decades of the Twentieth Century

Decades	*Number of Studies*	*Number of Findings*
Data not given	6	88
1910–1919	2	2
1920–1929	2	11
1930–1939	0	0
1940–1949	23	294
1950–1959	13	105
1960–1969	17	315
1970–1979	125	1,645
1980–1984	115	1,648
Total	**303**	**4,108**

Source : Brun, 1985

Eighty seven per cent of the total findings were from studies conducted in North America, while such studies from other parts of the world are scant. In the Indian context and in other developing countries where the need is great the dearth of nutrition education research is strongly felt.

Of the total findings stated above, seventeen per cent of them were from studies where random sampling was adopted. Twenty two per cent however were from studies in which subjects were randomly assigned to conditions, control group was included in sixty four per cent of them while the remaining had no control. These observations indicate the increasing realisation of purposive sampling and control as crucial to research in nutrition education.

Nineteen per cent of the findings were from studies containing national samples while fifty seven per cent contained only local samples. Participants varied widely on sex, age, economic status and cultural background. The reviewer, Brun (1985) was of the opinion that the findings of this meta-analysis, have wide applicability.

Studies related to the current problem were reviewed and presented under the following sub-headings :

— Studies on Knowledge of Nutrition

— Studies on attitudes toward Nutrition

— Studies on practices of Nutrition

— Studies on Food Beliefs

— Correlations among Nutrition Knowledge, Attitude and Practice

— Relationship of Knowledge, Attitude, Personality Traits and Nutrition Related Behaviour

— Studies on Socio-Economic Status, Attitudes and Knowledge

Studies on Knowledge of Nutrition

Young et al., (1956) reported on what the home makers know about nutrition. He found that actual performance of the home-maker in feeding her family was found to be considerably better than her theoretical knowledge on the subject. However, the food groups about which knowledge was weakest were also most poorly used. The adequacy of food used was related to nutritional knowledge.

Mothers nutrition knowledge was studied by Devadas et al., in 1967 while conducting an investigation on 99 pre-schoolers who come from 82 rural families. A diet survey was conducted to elicit the information on feeding pre-school children. Mothers were tested for their nutrition knowledge in relation to their education, caste, occupation and the nutritional status of their children. Results revealed that the socio-economic factors tested did not have much influence on the mothers knowledge related to feeding practices of children.

A study was done by Emmons and Hayes (1973) on the nutritional knowledge of mothers and children. An attempt was made to see how many mothers practice what they reported as important in their children's diet. The results revealed that the nutrition practices seemed on the whole much better than nutrition knowledge might indicate. This was true with all food groups except vegetables. While, 88 to 87 per cent of the mothers said vegetables were important in their child's diet, only 55 to 69 per cent actually reported vegetables in their child's diet on the day of the recall. Further more, only 36 to 54 per cent of the children reported having vegetables in their diet on that same day. These observations indicated that the mother's practices were not based on an understanding of what they were doing.

Vijayadurgamba and Geervani (1974) made an attempt to assess the dietary pattern and nutritional status of pre-school children in relation to their mother's awareness of nutritional knowledge living in urban slums of Hyderabad. Most of the mothers were unaware of the right type of feeding practices of infancy and pre-school age and are generally led by customs and beliefs. Eighty eight per cent of mothers belong to the poor category of nutritional awareness.

Smith et al., (1986) conducted a study to determine the effectiveness of the supplemental food programme for women, infants and children (WIC) for mothers and their anaemic children under five years of age. The interventions for the experimental group included individual counselling, group nutrition classes and provision of WIC food vouchers for purchasing foods containing essential nutrients that were deficient in the diets of this high risk population. The parents, guardians were also counselled on meal planning, shopping for food and food storage and preparations. Each child's diet was assessed after 6 months. The 30 minute education classes consisted of audio-visual presentations followed by discussions. Subjects like the importance of breast feeding, of infant nutrition, of childhood nutrition and of consuming adequate amounts of vitamin A and C, Iron and Protein and Calcium were presented. The results of the 24 hour dietary assessment in the experimental group at the end of the study showed that the intake of 8 per cent of the participants were still below the RDA (Required Daily Allowance) for vitamin A, while 4 per cent were below RDA for Iron and Folacin. The vitamin C and protein intakes were adequate. The difference in the mean pre and post test results of participants in the educational presentation indicated an increase in their knowledge on each subject, with the greatest difference in the pre and post tests for the vitamins A and C presence. Intervention process affected the outcome in a statistically significant way.

Nagwekar (1972) conducted a study in a village of Gujarat State to identify educational needs of rural mothers with regard to nutrition for children of 0–5 years. She found that the average knowledge of the mothers in child nutrition was below 50 per cent of the total knowledge considered essential for these mothers. This study indicates the need for education in nutrition among rural mothers. Nagwekar also reported that the aged members of the family were in greater need of nutrition education. Venkatachalam et al., (1965) found that the nutrition knowledge of school children was very poor.

Naidu (1981) found that among the rural people in Andhra Pradesh, only 30.66 per cent and 28.66 per cent of the experimental and controlled groups respectively had the knowledge of locally available nutritious foods. 41.33 per cent and 36 per cent of the controlled and experimental groups respectively had knowledge about the essential foods to be consumed daily.

Carruth et al., (1971) conducted a study to find out the increase and retention of knowledge by cartoon approach in nutrition education. The knowledge mean scores on pre-test, post-test and retention test obtained by experimental group were 72.38, 84.05 and 80.99 respectively. The subjects showed a significant increase in knowledge after the exposure to nutrition education. The retention test scores revealed that the amount of information lost during the six weeks time lapse was not statistically significant.

Age and Knowledge of Nutrition

Gupta (1981) reported that the awareness about the personal hygiene, balanced diet and eating was significantly higher in the students of lower age groups as compared to the students of higher age groups. Also, Sims (1976) found out the correlation between age and nutritional knowledge. Lower age groups had better knowledge of nutrition than upper age groups. It was found statistically significant at 0.01 level. Usha Devi (1983) found that age of the organisers had no effect on their nutritional knowledge. Whereas Sudha Rani (1987) found that age of the organiser has influence on the total nutritional knowledge, that is organisers aged 23 years and below have more knowledge than those aged above 23 years.

Occupation and Knowledge of Nutrition

Direct relationship exists between nutritional knowledge and occupation. Higher occupational groups had better knowledge of nutrition than the lower occupational groups (Sims, 1976).

Family Type and Knowledge of Nutrition

Gupta (1981) reported that awareness of eating practices was observed to be somewhat higher in the adolescents belonging to nuclear families. However, no significant differences were found in the nuclear and joint family adolescents on the degree of awareness of balanced diet in the study.

Family Size and Knowledge of Nutrition

Sims (1976) reported that family size was negatively related to nutritional knowledge. Families with small size had better nutritional knowledge than families with large size. The difference was found to be significant in this study at the 0.01 level.

Income and Knowledge of Nutrition

Sims (1976) found that there was a positive and higher correlation between nutritional knowledge of mothers and their family income. Higher income groups had more knowledge than the lower income groups. This result was found significant at 0.01 level. Gupta (1981) reported that awareness of eating practices among the students of higher income groups was found to be significantly higher. It was also found in the study that the awareness of balanced diet between the groups of adolescents from higher and lower income groups was not significant.

Usha Devi (1983) and Sudha Rani (1987) found that income of the organisers has no relation to the total nutritional knowledge possessed by them.

Educational Status and Knowledge of Nutrition

Usha Devi (1983) and Sudha Rani (1987) reported that educational status of the organisers is not related to their nutritional knowledge. That is, there exists no difference in the total nutritional knowledge between organisers with educational qualification of 10th fail and below and 10th pass and above.

Sex and Knowledge of Nutrition

Usha Devi (1983) found that both male and female organisers have equal amount of nutritional knowledge. But Sudha Rani (1987) reported that female organisers have more knowledge compared to male organisers.

Caste and Knowledge of Nutrition

Sudha Rani (1987) found that organisers belonging to Forward Caste have more knowledge than those belonging to Non-Forward Caste.

Marital Status and Knowledge of Nutrition

Usha Devi (1983) found that marital status of the organisers had no effect on the total nutritional knowledge possessed by them. But the study of Sudha Rani (1987) indicated that married organisers are more knowledgeable than unmarried organisers.

Studies on Attitude Towards Nutrition

Summers (1970) and Perry (1976) independently proved that attitudes have the quality of motivation. Attitudes were found not only to contribute to routinizing behaviour, but also have a directional quality. In that directional quality, they involve an affective dimension such as person's evaluation of liking for or emotional response to the attitude object. For instance, Baker (1972) reported the influence of a teacher's negative attitude on the subsequent selection of squash by her elementary-age pupils. Her negative attitude towards squash resulted in similar behaviour by the children.

Perkins et al., (1980) studied the relationship between the teachers' and students' attitudes related to nutrition at the school level. Positive significant relationship was found between the nutritional attitudes of teachers and students. These attitudes also lead to nutritional behaviour in both the cases.

The above studies reveal that attitude is one of the important factors influencing the food behaviour of individuals.

Religion and Attitude Towards Nutrition

Arora et al., (1973) reported that different religious groups had different attitudes, taboos and beliefs with respect to certain foods. Rice, Curds, Banana and Orange were considered to induce cold by over 90 per cent of the Hindu and Jain mothers. Two-thirds of Muslims, Christians and Sikh mothers reported that meat and egg were supposed to be 'hot' foods among non-vegetarians and onions among Jains. Over one and half of the Muslim mothers and a lesser proportion of mothers in other religions believed that consumption of sugar resulted in worm infestation. 'Massordal' (Lentil) was considered a cause of joint pains and indigestion by Jain mothers who avoided its cooking in view of its resemblances to the colour of flesh.

Occupation and Attitude Towards Nutrition

Muthaiah (1972) found a direct and a significant relationship between nutritional attitudes and occupation.

Income and Attitude Towards Nutrition

Muthayya (1972) found that nutritional attitudes were directly related to income.

Studies on Practices of Nutrition

Good nutrition is a basic component of health. The essentials that constitute balance diet are (1) milk and milk products, (2) egg/fish/meat, (3) green leafy vegetables, (4) vegetables, (5) pulses and cereals and (6) fruits. Many studies revealed that the nutritional status of the rural population is very poor. Despite the availability of certain foods (occasionally and freely/cheaply) many of the rural people are not using them. Venkatachalam et al., (1965) found that 60.25 per cent students did not consume milk, which therefore, meant a lack of balanced nutrition.

Prasad et al., (1969) reported that all the villagers near Lucknow washed their hands with water before taking their meals, but children were seen seldom washing their hand, before eating.

The Department of International Health, John Hopkins University School of Hygiene and Public Health (1976) reported that in Turkey a study was conducted with a sample of 528 women pertaining to their maternal and child nutrition practices. It was found in this study that 46 per cent of the respondents reported no change from the normal diet and of the remaining 54 per cent (283 women) 40 per cent espoused light foods, and 14 per cent noted a variety of other items.

Pratt (1976) summarizing the results of some studies pertaining to nutritional practices of 7,500 families in 1955–66 concluded that there was a failure to consume essential nutrients and also a tendency to consume unnecessary or harmful foods on the part of the families. The proportion of families with good diets dropped from 60 per cent in 1955 to 50 per cent in 1965, calcium deficiency was due to declining use of milk, while vitamin A and C deficiency were attributed to insufficient consumption of fresh vegetables and fruits and the tendency to skip some meals was partly responsible for these deficiencies.

Age and Practice of Nutrition

Jelso et al. (1965) found a negative correlation between age and practice of nutrition.

Ferry (1981) after analysing the findings of many studies conducted in different countries reported that the older the women, the longer the breast feeding duration they had. It was found in this analysis that the magnitude of the relationship varied in countries. The countries analysed with their means in the parentheses were listed below.

Bangladesh (24.1), Indonesia (19.5), Jordan (9.3), Republic of Korea (15.7), Malaysia (4.5), Nepal (20.6), Pakistan (16.1), Philippines (10.9), Sri Lanka (14.7), Thailand (14.0), Colombia (7.0), Costa Rica (4.5), Dominican Republic (8.4), Guyana (7.6), Jamaica (7.4), Mexico (8.7), Panama (6.6), and Peru (10.8).

The Haiti Fertility Survey (1977) reported that the mean duration of breast feeding tended to increase with the age of mother. A greater proportion of younger women had never breast-fed. Nearly 40 per cent of women under 25 years did not breast feed as compared to less than 20 per cent of women aged 35 years and above.

The Sri Lanka Fertility Survey (1975) reported that older women tended to report longer duration of breast feeding than women aged less than 25 years, the mean duration decreased to 19.4 months for older women and to 14.2 months for the younger ones. The findings of the Pakistan Fertility and Family Survey (1974), the Colombia Fertility Survey (1976), the Korean National Fertility Survey (1974), the Sudan Fertility Survey (1979), the Peru Fertility Survey (1977), the Keny Fertility Survey (1977), and the Jordan Fertility Survey (1976) revealed similar trends.

But the Bangladesh Fertility Survey (1975) reported that there was a close similarity of results for different age groups with regard to breast feeding. Mosley et al., (1982) found that among women aged 25-34, the practice of breast feeding was limited.

Religion and Practice of Nutrition

Arora et al., (1973) found that Christians and Hindus introduce solid foods at the earliest rather than Muslims.

Caste and Practice of Nutrition

Datta (1977) reported that the low caste people prolong breast feeding for a longer duration than higher caste people. Also, Venkatachalam et al., (1971), Mukherji (1969), Anand et al., (1962), Rao (1957), Seth et al., (1970), Mehta et al., (1972), Bhandari et al., (1973), Walia et al., (1974), Thaman et al., (1964), Thaman et al., (1968), Saxena et al., (1968), Ghai et al, (1971), Someswra Rao et al, (1959), Madhavi et al., (1973), Puri et al., (1976), reported the same fact through their investigation. Rani (1982) found that 80 per cent of the Scheduled Castes and 77 per cent of the non-Scheduled Caste women were breast feeding in villages.

Occupation and Practice of Nutrition

Jelso et al., (1965) found that nutritional practice was directly related to occupation.

Mosely et al., (1982) reported that the practice of breast feeding was 15 months among the wives whose husbands were professionals or who had white collar jobs, while the practice of breast feeding was 18 months among the wives whose husbands work in traditional agrarian occupation or as household servants. Also, the findings of the Sudan Fertility Survey (1979) reported the same fact.

Ferry et al., (1983) reported that the length of breast feeding among the wives of farm workers was very much longer than the mean for the whole country. Very short duration of breast feeding was found among wives of white collar workers. Several studies done in India by Venkatachalam et al., (1971), Mukherji (1969), Anand et al., (1962), Rao (1957), Seth et al., (1970), Mehta et al., (1972), Bhandari et al., (1973), Walia et al., (1974), Thaman et al., (1964), Thaman et al., (1968), Saxena et al., (1968), Ghai et al., (1971), Someswara Raò et al., (1959), Madhavi et al., (1973) and Puri et al., (1976) revealed that breast feeding was prolonged for longer duration by the lower occupational groups than the higher occupational groups.

Number of Children and Practice of Nutrition

Rao (1971) reported that families with three or less children were observed to have better intake of calories and protein than families with four or more children. The difference in calorie intake per adult unit between families with three or less children and those with four or more children was nearly 300. The difference in protein intake was of the order of 10 grams daily.

Tomar et al., (1980) found a negative and inverse relationship between protein intake and parity among the industrial worker families. The protein intake (gms. consumption unit per day) decreased fastly as the number of family members increased.

Income and Practice of Nutrition

Jelso et al., (1965) reported that there was direct relationship between income and nutritional practices.

Arora et al., (1973) found that breast feeding was prolonged for longer duration by poorer families than rich. Datta Banik (1977), Venkatachalam et al., (1971), Mukherji (1969), Anand et al., (1962), Rao (1957), Seth et al., (1970), Mehta et al., (1972), Bhandari et al., (1973), Walia et al., (1974), Thaman et al., (1964), Thaman et al., (1968), Saxena et al., (1968), Ghai et al., (1971), Someswara et al., (1959), Madhavi et al., (1973) and Puri et al., (1978) found similar trends in their studies. But Sharma et al., (1977) reported that there was no relationship between income and breast feeding.

Datta Banik (1977) reported that the higher socio-economic classes started supplementary food at about 6 months of age whereas most of the mothers from the lower socio-economic classes started supplementary feeding after one year of age. But Gupta et al., (1979) found that there was no relationship between income and weaning. Also, Sharma et al., (1977) found that there was no relationship between income and supplementary feeding of children in urban areas of Sindhi population.

Education and Practice of Nutrition

Alford and Tibbets (1971) found that education increased the consumption of vegetables by children.

Jelso et al., (1965) found that nutritional practices were directly related to education. But Ismail et al., (1975) reported that mothers with education upto 5 years of schooling were not better in nutritional practices than illiterate mothers.

Ferry and David P. Smith (1983) reported that in Kenya, Lesotho Senegal, Sudan (north), Jordan, Syria, Bangladesh, Nepal, Pakistan, Sri Lanka, Indonesia, Republic of Korea, Malaysia, Philippines, Thailand, Colombia, Paraguay, Peru, Venezuela, Costa Rica, Mexico, Panama, Dominican Republic, Haiti, Jamaica, Trinidad and Tobago, the length of breast feeding decreased as the duration of education level increased. Among women with 1–3 years of education, there was a decrease in breast feeding of about 1–2 months as compared to women with no education.

The Haiti Fertility Survey (1977) reported that the mean length of breast-feeding varied greatly according to the level of education from 11.3 months for women with no education to 9.7 months for women with primary education and 4.4 months for women with secondary or higher education. Also, the Sudan Fertility Sruvey (1979), the Peru Fertility Survey (1977), the Kenya Fertility Survey (1978), the Fiji Fertility Survey (1974), the Pakistan Fertility Sruvey (1975), the Colombia Fertility Survey (1976), and the Korean Fertility Survey (1974) revealed similar trends of results.

Puri et al., (1976) found that illiterate mothers gave prolonged breast feeding till the age of 16.6 months while it was 10.2 months for educated mothers. Also, Narayana et al., (1974), Ghosh et al., (1976), Datta Banik (1977), Venkatachalam et al., (1971), Mukherji (1969), Anand et al., (1962), Rao (1957), Seth et al., (1970), Mehta et al., (1972), Bhandari et al., (1973), Walia et al., (1974), Thaman et al., (1964), Thaman et al., (1968), Saxena et al., (1968), Madhavi et al., (1973), Arora et al., (1973) and Awastha et al., (1983) found similar trends of results.

But the Bangladesh Fertility Survey (1975) reported that there was no such difference between various educational groups with regard to breast feeding.

Arora et al., (1973) reported that maternal literacy was more closely related to early onset of breast feeding than parental literacy. A statistically significant observation was that the level of literacy was associated with the incidence of schedule feeding. Also, the education introduce solid foods at an early age than the illiterates.

Studies on Food Beliefs

Brown et al., (1963) found that house wives have some nutritional beliefs in U.S.A., but, these beliefs do not necessarily influence their food purchases.

Storrer (1977) conducted a survey in Baroda, India and commented that "why people eat and what they eat depend upon what local foods are available, on ability to import food and on personal economy, but this is not all". She observed that peoples' beliefs about food have an important influence on food behaviour which constitutes food selection/preparation, serving and consumption. These beliefs may be religious, traditional, medicinal or Pseudo Scientific in origin.

Storrer said that there are several different food belief systems operating through out the world and one which is widely distributed in varying forms is that of 'hot' and 'cold' foods. This classification has been observed in South America, Central America, Malaya, Pakistan, some Mediterranean countries, the Sahara, Philippines, China and in India. These beliefs in many parts of the world are of ancient origin.

In India, by tradition, it is the women who have acquired the skills and assimilated the beliefs governing food and its preparation. Hence, the information on 'hot' and 'cold' concept and its application was obtained from women.

The data revealed that the 'hot' foods were said to produce giddiness, thirst, fatigue, sweating, inflammatory reactions and accelerated effect on digestion. The 'cold' foods were said to cause cheerfulness and pleasure of mind, to sustain life and to impart strength and steadiness to the body. Cereals, pulses, green leafy vegetables, other vegetables, milk and milk products and fruits were said to be 'cold' foods while fleshy foods and spices were labelled as 'hot' foods. Oils and roots and tubers were distributed in both the categories. Regarding the application of beliefs, 'hot' foods were avoided during pregnancy and 'cold' foods during lactation. During infancy and childhood certain of both 'hot' and 'cold' were avoided. During fever time 'hot' foods were avoided and 'cold' foods during cough and cold.

The author concluded that to the Indian communities, food beliefs are not idle superstition but concepts which are important and meaningful to them especially during physiological stress. Such beliefs are often disregarded by nutrition educators which means that dietary advice given by them may well be ignored. Therefore, they need to have deeper understanding of belief systems and act accordingly.

Devadas (1968) reported that the concept of 'hot' and 'cold' is not in terms of the temperature sense, but in the sense that some foods are believed to produce heat in the body. Similarly 'cold' foods produce a cooling effect in the body. Therefore, 'hot' foods are considered suitable for certain conditions like lactation, cold and stomach pain. Cold foods are good for certain conditions such as fever, pregnancy, etc. A few of both 'hot' and 'cold' foods are recommended and a few of them are avoided during specific conditions.

Correlations among Nutrition Knowledge, Attitude and Practices

In most research and evaluation studies in nutrition education, one finds that knowledge, attitude and behaviour are the common variables being measured The foundations for this focus are strongly supported in educational theory.

Nutrition education is aimed at influencing the knowledge, attitudes and behaviour related to nutrition. These three outcomes of nutrition education are related. Although several socio-psychological theories state that knowledge, attitude and behaviour should be consistent (Insko and Schopler, 1967), a number of studies indicate that their relationships are not simple or automatic (Wicker, 1969; Swanson, 1972; Liska, 1979).

The relationships among knowledge, attitude and behaviour are more intricate. Behaviour typically has multiple causes. The view that nutrition knowledge and attitudes will determine nutrition behaviour simplifies the complexity involved in food selection, preparation and consumption. Behaviour is mostly determined by many motivations operating at the same time, therefore food behaviour is usually the result of many motivations rather than one. Most individuals value health and so it is assumed that they will adopt a life style commensurate with assuring lasting health. Whether they do or not, depends upon internal influences such as nutrition knowledge, attitudes, personality traits and anxiety depression and external factors like socio-cultural expectations, food availability, cost of food, advertising appeals, food popularity and a desire to keep with the peers. Despite the fact that external factors may determine the immediate behaviour than do internal influences, the degree to which knowledge, attitudes and behaviour are related has been the subject of considerable debate. Brun (1985) also emphasized the above view points and expressed the same opinion based on his extensive review related to nutrition education.

In this context, Pelto and Pelto (1978) and Kolasa et al., (1979) and Kolasa (1981) encouraged researchers to study the knowledge, attitudes, beliefs and practices of individuals and groups. Glanz (1981) said that it is very important to evaluate the intervening variables such as knowledge, attitudes and beliefs presumed to be related to improved nutritional behaviour.

Knowledge and Attitude

Eppright et al., (1970) reported a study on nutrition knowledge and attitudes of mothers. Mothers of pre-school children in 12 States were interviewed regarding the eating behaviour of their children and certain family characteristics. Each mother was asked to record a 3 day food intake for her child. The results of the study indicated that nutrition knowledge and attitudes towards meal planning, food preparation, nutrition and permissiveness in feeding children were interrelated factors influencing the quality of the diets of pre-school children to varying degrees.

Peterson and Kies (1972) conducted a study in the State of Nebraska to determine the nutrition knowledge, attitudes and the relationship of knowledge and attitudes of Kinder Garten I, II & III grade class teachers. Simple linear correlations were used to determine the relationship between knowledge scores and attitude of the teachers. The correlation was 0.04 which was significant at 10 per cent level.

It is generally believed that greater knowledge of nutrition will result in more desirable attitudes toward nutrition education. However, the presented data in this study revealed that little relationship existed between knowledge of nutrition and favourable attitudes towards teaching nutrition. These findings suggested that a greater knowledge of nutrition will not necessarily increase the probability that teachers will develop more positive attitude towards teaching nutrition. Here, the attitudes have been reported to influence behaviour, independent of the individuals knowledge of nutritional concepts and practices.

Similar to the findings of Hays and Emmons (1973), some findings were reported by Baker (1972) and Lewin (1943). This may be temporary which is likely to be confirmed soon with other associated factors like attitudes and knowledge.

In contrast to the above studies, Weigel (1976) reported that attitudes cannot influence the practice unless it is assisted with adequate knowledge.

Knowledge and Practice

Ismail et al., (1975) conducted a study to find out the association between mothers formal education and their nutritional knowledge and practices and the growth pattern of their children. The mothers were divided into four groups based on their schooling. Nutritional knowledge as well as practices were evaluated using a nutritional knowledge test and a questionnaire. The results indicated that majority of the mothers in all groups scored poorly on the knowledge test and on the practice questionnaire. Mothers upto 5 years of schooling are not better in their knowledge or practice than illiterate mothers. Though the group which has 7, 8 or 9 years of schooling had better knowledge and practices they were still deficient in knowledge and poor in practices specifically in those areas related to infant feeding.

Phillips et al., (1978) studied a group of mothers of pre-school children for their nutritional knowledge and use of food in daily living. Thirty upper middle class mothers and their pre-school children were interviewed to study the effect that food and nutrition knowledge of the mothers had on the use of pre-schoolers and families with no older children. In the first group, the mothers food and nutrition knowledge was positively associated with behaviour regarding the use of pre-sweetened cereals. In the second group where there were oldest children in the family, the mothers food and nutrition knowledge was not related to their cereal purchasing behaviour. The food and nutrition knowledge test scores for both groups were similar.

Krause and Fox (1977) investigated the factors influencing the nutrition knowledge and attitudes of physicians practicing medicine in the University of Nebraska utilizing a mail survey technique. The assumption that physicians had gained a bulk of their nutrition knowledge by way of post-graduate study and experience was not supported by the findings. A significant negative relationship (P 0.05) was found between the nutritional knowledge and the years of practice.

Devadas and Co-workers (1977) reported a study on the "Nutritional Knowledge and Practices of the Rural Home Makers in a Post-ANP and Non-Post ANP Block". Fifteen villages in Coimbatore district where nutrition education had been given for one year under the Applied Nutrition Programme and 15 villages without nutrition education were compared. The criteria for the assessment was the details regarding food production, consumption and food expenditure patterns, food beliefs and dietary practices, willingness and enthusiasm of the home makers to participate in the community activities and their nutritional knowledge. The study indicates that the mothers belonging to the post-ANP Block have more nutritional knowledge than mothers belonging to the non-ANP Block.

Vasanthakumari (1979) conducted "A Study of the Relationship Between Nutritional Knowledge and Practice of Rural Mothers to that of the Dietary Quality and Nutritional Status of Their Children". Significant relationship was found between the knowledge and practice of mothers in control group. There was no significant relationship between the two in experimental group.

Lovett et al., (1970) studied the impact of nutrition education programme on second grade level school children in terms of their knowledge and practices. The nutrition education was for a duration of six months. The nutrition education was for a duration of six months. Pre-test and post-test was the methodology used for evaluation. The experimental group showed significant increase both in knowledge (360 per cent) and practices (150 per cent). From these findings, the authors implied that knowledge definitely contributes to practices but, to a limited extent (50 per cent).

Alford and Tibbets (1971) conducted a study to prove that "nutrition education increases the consumption of vegetables by children". In the first camp session, 71 children (experimental group) were observed for vegetable eating practices and given an educational programme on "importance of vegetables in the diet". The consumption was recorded before and after education. A control group was also kept without giving nutrition education. Vegetable consumption increased significantly in the experimental group. From these findings, it can be concluded that increase in knowledge results in increase in practices.

In contrast to the above studies Amudson (1956) reported that nutritonal knowledge did not influence the nutrition practices.

Bell and Lamb (1973) studied the influence of nutrition education on the eating practices of Vth grade students, and the six weeks instructional module on dietary modification and cognitive learning of 1,500 V grade students in 33 randomly selected schools of five States. Post-test was administered to the experimental group which indicated that the above group had significantly higher post-test mean score than that of the control group at 0.01 level.

After another six weeks during which period neither group received any treatment, when the retention test was administered, the mean scores were the same as those of the immediate post-test. It is concluded that the nutritional knowledge is documented as a factor influencing nutrition related behaviour of modification.

Hoorweg and McDowell (1979) reported on the impact of nutrition education conducted in Africa. The results indicated that desired changes in nutrition knowledge, in food preferences and in better recognition of symptoms of malnutrition were observed.

Devadas et al., (1974) reported the findings of nutrition education conducted in four primary schools. One school was provided with school lunch alone, second school with nutrition education through curriculum alone, third school with school lunch along with nutrition education through curriculum and fourth school served as control. The programme lasted for a period of six months. The authors compared the nutrition knowledge and practices adopted by their mothers in turn. School lunch programme combined with the nutrition education curriculum had a significantly higher beneficial effect than the curriculum alone.

Devadas et al., (1979) studied the impact of a nutrition and child care programme on fifty mothers over a period of five months. The impact was measured in terms of nutrition knowledge and dietary practices of mothers. The nutrition knowledge scores of the participating mothers were significantly higher than the scores of the control group of mothers and promising changes were not observed in dietary practices compared to that of knowledge.

Devadas et al., (1982) evaluated and reported the impact of a nutrition education programme which lasted for a six months period. The target group was 130 members of women's clubs in selected villages. The women were directed towards economically and nutritionally beneficial activities. This intervention programme improved the mothers nutritional practices. In the same year Devadas (1982) conducted an education project designed to develop awareness about food, health and sanitary practices. The target group consisted of fifty women and 100 children from rural areas. The health and sanitary practices of women and children participated were improved. Another study was done by Devadas and Co-workers (1982) to assess the effectiveness of a nutrition education programme which lasted for six months. The participants were 50 home makers. Positive results were observed.

Devadas (1986) conducted a base line survey among 2,900 households drawn from two slums and six community development blocks, Tamil Nadu, India. Based on the findings of the survey, priority concepts in nutrition and health education and environmental sanitation were identified. These concepts were incorporated into the existing elementary school curriculum and suitable instructional materials were developed for all the 6,000 teachers from the 660 primary schools in the selected area. The orientation training was conducted by instructors who had bachelor's degrees in education and master's degrees in nutrition. The trained primary school teachers, in turn, taught the nutrition and health and environmental sanitation lessons in their classes. Evaluative criteria were knowledge of children and teachers, practices of the mothers and the anthropometric and clinical status of the children. Children for evaluation were restricted only to classes 3–5.

Significant changes in knowledge were observed in both the groups of teachers and children. Training given to teachers was proved to be promising. Positive changes occurred in the practices of the mothers of primary school children. Reduction of nutritional deficiency symptoms was observed. In view of the encouraging results, author suggested for further expansion of the programme throughout the country.

Aforesaid findings in the Indian context, indicate that nutrition knowledge is one of the potent factors influencing nutritional behaviour. But the nutritional behaviour of the people is not encouraging. This might be due to the limited scope the lay people have to nutrition information sources such as mass communication.

Thus in India nutrition education programmes have demonstrated that a higher percentage of knowledge gain is possible than the change in practices. Very little attention is being paid to improve the attitudes towards nutrition and also to assess the attitudes. These findings reflect that the methodology adopted for nutrition education is not suitable to bring about changes in attitudes and practices to a great extent. This generalisation was supported by Whitehead (1973) who reviewed nutrition education research in the worldwide context.

Hochbaum (1979) and (1980), Yankelovich (1978), Sims (1981) stated that nutrition educators have falsely assumed that lack of nutrition knowledge prevents people from choosing foods wisely. Hochbaum (1981) reported that nutrition education in general is still shaped by three largely invalid assumptions : (1) awareness of the health effects of nutrition is a potent motivation for people to regulate their food intake; (2) lack of nutrition knowledge that prevents people from eating more rationally and (3) informed people will eat more rationally as long as they can afford and have access to proper nutrition. However, there is ample and convincing evidence that knowledge of good nutrition by itself has only limited, if any, effect on nutrition related behaviour.

Social Scientists, nutrition and health educators are becoming increasingly aware that the attainment of knowledge does not necessarily result in the modification of the behaviour of individuals.

The process through which nutrition education affects nutrition knowledge, attitudes and behaviour begins with nutrition information being presented to participants. Presenting information does not mean that the information will be attended to learned, retained or applied. Knowledge does not, in and of itself, cause changes in behaviour or even attitudes except under a very limited set of condition (Watson and Johnson, 1972). In many cases people do not assign weight to information in strict accordance with its importance (Hogarth, 1981; Kahneman and Tversky, 1979; Nisbett and Ross, 1980; Tversky and Kahneman, 1974). Being informed does not mean that people will act intelligently in promoting heath and preventing disease. Information is often disregarded, altered and used to justify and rationalize current behaviour rather than to stimulate behavioural changes. It needs prior education to effectively interpret and use information.

Attitude and Practice

Since attitudes are thought to be pre-dispositives to action (Mcclintock, 1972), the failure to find a high correlation between attitudes and behaviour in early social psychological research was frustrating (Wicker, 1969; Fishbein and Ajzen, 1972). Nutrition educators have shared this frustration as the correlations between nutrition related attitudes and behaviour have been found to range from approximately 0.01 to 0.55 in studies that sampled different populations, attitudes and behaviours. In energy food consumption research, attitudinal variables have indicated little association with energy food consumption (McDougall et al., 1981 and Ritchie et al., 1981). Millions of people aspire to heath are aware of the link between well-balanced means and health, and can afford to, yet still persist in undesirable practices.

Knowledge, Attitude and Practice

Schwartz (1975) investigated the nature of relationship of nutritional knowledge to attitudes and practices and the inter-relationship of knowledge and attitudes with practices among the subjects. He employed the knowledge-attitude-practices (K-A-P) model adopted from the cognitive-affective-behaviour theory or attitude-behaviour relationship in the field of social psychology. The target population involved was 1969 female graduates selected from Ohio High Schools.

Data were analysed to determine which of the four models describe the inter-relationship of nutrition knowledge, attitudes and practices of the graduates. The following are the four possible models of the inter-relationship of nutrition knowledge, attitudes and practices.

K—A—P Model I K⟷A⟷P

K—A—P Model II K, A → P

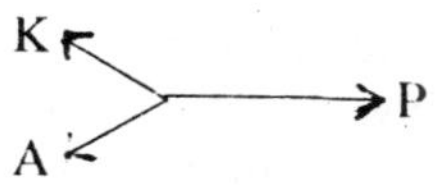

K—A—P Model III K ⟷ P, A ⟷ P

K—A—P Model IV K ⟷ A, A ⟷ P, K ⟷ P

K = Knowledge; A = Attitude; P = Practices

Model I	:	Attitudes mediate knowledge and practices
Model II	:	Knowledge and attitudes interact to influence practices
Model III	:	Knowledge and attitudes independently influence practices
Model IV	:	Knowledge influence practices both directly and indirectly as mediated by attitudes concurrently.

The findings supported the Model I, i.e., relationship of knowledge to attitude and attitude to practices but do not support direct relationship between nutritional knowledge and practices. It is evident from the study that the knowledge influences the attitude and in turn the attitudes influence the practices. However in communities with a different background a different model may be working. Further research along these lines is essential for developing group specific nutrition education programme.

Brun (1985) computed calculations for both effect size and 'Z' scores. The results are presented in Table 2.2. Significant relationship exist between nutrition knowledge and behaviour as seen by statistically significant (P = 0.02) correlations. The relation between nutrition attitude and behaviour is also significant, as indicated by the Z-score correlation. The relation between nutrition knowledge and attitude did not reach statistical significance.

Thus there has been mixed evidence as to whether or not knowledge, attitudes and behaviour are related. The relationship among the three variables is considered to be complex and incompletely understood. Nutrition education research focuses on signifi-

Table 2.2 : Correlation Among Nutrition Knowledge, Attitude and Behaviour

Variables	*Correlation*	*Number*	*Significance level (P)*
Knowledge and Attitude : Effect Size	0.17	29	0.19
Knowledge and Behaviour : Effect Size	0.50	38	0.001
Attitude and Behaviour : Effect Size	0.20	23	0.18
Knowledge and Attitude : Z-score	0.09	35	0.31
Attitude and Behaviour : Z-Score	0.47	28	0.006

Source : Brun, 1985.

cant relationships between nutrition knowledge and behaviour as well as nutrition attitudes and behaviour. These outcomes will be of interest to nutrition educators and social psychologists involved in attitude modification and change.

Studies on the Relationship of Knowledge, Attitude, Personality Traits and Nutrition Related Behaviours

Carruth et al., (1977) determined whether or not a significant relationship existed among nutritional knowledge, attitudes, personality traits and nutrition related behaviours. Respondents were selected purposively from Missouri's Expanded Food and Nutrition Education Programme. The experimental group received five weeks training on weight modification concepts. Both experimental and control groups were pre and post tested for their knowledge and practices. Direct observations were made of only experimental group's nutritional practices. Cattell and Eber's sixteen personality factor questionnaire (Form E) was used to characterize them either as adoptable (flexible) and or as self-opinionated (rigid). Carruth's attitude questionnaire was used to measure their adoptability toward changing nutritional practices.

The data indicated that the training resulted in a significant positive gain in nutrition knowledge. Nutrition knowledge was not significantly correlated with nutrition behaviour. Same relation was observed between attitudes—change proneness and behaviour. Significant negative relation was obtained between age, a personal factor and nutritional behaviour. Further, multivariable analysis documented that nutrition knowledge was not as potent a predictor of nutritional behaviour as were attitudes, personality traits and age.

Reddy and Chandralekha (1978) studied the relative influence of certain selected factors on the nutritional practices of rural mothers of pre-schoolers. Sixty respondents were selected purposively from the target group of OXFAM Project, Department of Home Science, S.V. University, Tirupati, Andhra Pradesh, India. Factors selected were nutrition knowledge, attitude, socio-cultural beliefs, socio-economic status, age and personality flexibility. Standard instruments were used to find out personality and socio-economic status. For other variables, instruments were devised.

The relationships between the nutritional practices and each of the selected factors were examined. The results were presented in Table 2.3. Nutritional practices were significantly related to knowledge, attitudes, socio-economic status, and socio-cultural beliefs. No significant relationship was found between the practices and age as

Table 2.3 : Interfactor Correlation Between Certain Variables and Nutritional Practices of Rural Mothers

Factors	*Knowledge*	*Attitude*	*Socio-economic status*	*Socio-cultural beliefs*	*Age*
Practices	0.71**	0.65**	0.33**	–0.58**	–0.22
Knowledge	--	0.71**	0.38**	–0.35**	–0.13
Attitude	--	--	0.37	–0.38**	–0.04
Socio-economic status	--	--	--	–0.06	--
Socio-cultural beliefs	--	--	--	--	–0.03

* Significant at 5 per cent level

** Significant at 1 per cent level

Source : Reddy and Chandralekha, 1978.

well as personality. Negative correlation was seen only between nutritional practices and socio-cultural beliefs and the rest were positive correlations. Regression equation revealed the relative intensity of influence of the significantly correlated variables. The pooled influence of four significant variables—knowledge, attitudes, socio-cultural beliefs and socio-economic status accounted 64.8 per cent of the variance while the remaining 35.2 per cent might be accounted for by unexplored factors. Out of 64.8 per cent, knowledge (29.2 per cent) and socio-cultural beliefs (20.2 per cent) had maximum influence and attitudes (12.8 per cent) and socio-economic status (2.6 per cent) came in that order. The reasons for this order may be many but the most significant ones are culture and procedural constraints/ limitations related to nutrition education and evaluation.

Sujatha (1981) conducted a similar study to explore the relationship amongst certain factors—nutrition knowledge, attitudes, socio-cultural beliefs, socio-economic status, personality and age. The respondents were rural mothers of pre-school children (70) from Chandragiri Block, Chittoor, Andhra Pradesh, India.

The results indicated that knowledge and socio-cultural beliefs were the most significant influencing factors to nutritional practices. Attitudes, age and socio-economic status followed next in that order of influence. Among the influences, negative influence was observed with regard to socio-cultural beliefs and age. There was no significant relation between personality and nutritional practices.

O'Connel et al., (1981) felt the role of teacher's attitude and beliefs toward nutrition in nutrition education as crucial. This feeling led them to assess nutrition—related attitudes and beliefs of teachers of Pennsylvania State, U.S.A. Valid instruments were used to measure their attitudes and beliefs toward nutrition. The results indicated that one group of teachers had high positive scores of attitudes and beliefs irrespective of their prior training in nutrition. The other group showed positive high scores only after training. The findings reveal that nutrition knowledge facilitates development of positive attitudes but cannot guarantee. This might be because attitudes have a strong base and backed by many social, cultural, personal and psychological factors, other than knowledge. Though it was predicted that positive attitudes of teachers lead to their better teaching in nutrition, this was not proved in present study. Explanation offered was that for many teachers' positive attitude was not accompanied by a personal willingness or interest in teaching nutrition. The author indicated that more research is needed to explore the possibilities of motivating such individuals.

Studies on Socio-economic Status, Attitudes and Knowledge

Sims (1976) examined the nutrition knowledge of a group of mothers of pre-school children in relation to selected demographic and attitudinal variables. The nutrition knowledge of respondents was measured using a test developed by Eppright and Co-workers (1970). Certain environmental factors both demographic and attitudinal were also measured and their relationships to nutrition knowledge were assessed.

Correlations between nutrition knowledge and selected attitude variables are presented in Table 2.4. The data reveal that the variables—socio-economic status, occupation, education and "nutrition is important" attitude were highly positively correlated with nutrition knowledge. The variables which were highly negatively related to nutrition knowledge were stage in life cycles, food dollars spent, total number of persons in home and "parents are all wise" and "powerlessness attitudes". These highly correlated factors were more important predictors of the nutrition knowledge than others. Moderate degree of relationship was observed between nutrition knowledge and income and 'equalitarianism' attitude. From the findings, it is evident that the mothers who possessed the highest level of nutrition knowledge were characterised by the following : higher socio-economic status, fewer persons in the house, young earlier stage in the family life cycle and less authoritarian and 'nutrition is important' attitude.

Menon and Prema (1977) conducted studies on attitudes of village women towards training in applied nutrition in National Extension Service (NES) blocks in Trivandrum District, Kerala. In this study the attitudes of respondents toward the training camps was statistically tested for significant associations in relation to their level of education, income, age and previous participation in similar camps. The analysis of variance of attitude scores indicate that the village women belonging to different educational status did not differ significantly in respect to their attitudes. The analysis of variance revealed that village women belonging to different income levels differed significantly in respect of their attitudes. This led to the conclusion

Table 2.4 : Correlation Between Nutrition Knowledge and Selected Demographic Attitude Variables

Demographic Variables	*Nutrition Knowledge*
1. Socio-economic status	0.53**
2. Occupation Education	0.51**
3. Income	0.20*
4. Stage in life cycle	–0.35**
5. Food dollars spent	–0.37**
6. Total person in home	–0.47**

Attitude Variables	*Nutrition Knowledge*
1. "Nutrition is Important" attitude	0.53**
2. "Equalitarianism" attitude	0.21**
3. "Parents are all wise" attitude	–0.42**
4. "Powerlessness" attitude	–0.42**

* Significant at 0.01 level
** Significant at 0.001 level

Source : Sims, 1976

that the higher the economic status more favourable were their attitudes. The group of upper socio-economic status indicated the most favourable attitude. The age of village women appeared to be positively and significantly related to the attitudes. The analysis of variance showed that the age group between 21 and 40 had significantly more favourable attitudes.

It is seen that the knowledge influences the attitudes and the attitudes in turn influence the practices. To bring about changes in nutritional practices, it is necessary to build up favourable attitudes through education, i.e., providing knowledge base by finding out the level and quality of existing knowledge and bringing the gap by suitable educational programmes. The present study is an attempt in this direction of locating the knowledge gap with a view to build up educational programmes and, hence, to change the nutritional practices.

The review also reveals that there are no studies directly relating to knowledge, attitudes and practices of Adult Education Programme Instructors Towards Nutrition. Hence, the present investigation is undertaken to identify the gap in the knowledge of nutrition and to study the influence of various socio-economic and demographic factors on knowledge, attitudes and practices of nutrition among adult education instructors in Andhra Pradesh.

3

Statement of the Problem, Hypotheses and Variables

India is a developing country, which occupies the second place in the world in terms of population. Most of the people are illiterate Hence in India, there is an increasing awareness of the problem of illiteracy and its effect on the economic, social and political development of the country. A wide diffusion of education is indispensable to modern civilization, and a high literacy rate is one of the most important indices of a highly developed economy. It is one of the demographic elements, which is a good measure of human progress towards modernization.

In a democracy, education is the only powerful instrument which can bring about a desirable change in its social, economic, cultural and political spheres. But such an education is neglected by a majority of our people in India.

Adult education is being conceived as a multisided effort to provide education facilities for adults. It would include literacy and fundamental education, vocational or job training education about nutrition and health consciousness and family problems as well as education about physical and personal development, literature, art, drama and other cultural items, community organisation, political and civil education, religious or economic education and a variety of other educational programmes designed primarily for adults.

Adult education is to help men and women to live fuller and richer lives in adjustment to their environment, to develop the best elements in their culture, and to achieve social and economic progress, which will enable them to take their rightful place in the modern world and to live together in peace.

Adult education seeks to enable the majority of our people to play an effective role as citizens and participate in various developmental programmes. Its programmes also seek to enable the bulk of our population to play an active role in bringing about 'socio-economic and cultural changes' so that social justice and equality are achieved.

The adult education programme for the economically productive age-group of 15–35 would pay rich dividends in terms of productivity, nutrition and health care, family planning and general betterment of the community leading to improvement in the quality of life. It was recognised that a socially-conscious, vigilant and literate community has a vital role in national development. In the words of Mrs. Indira Gandhi, "Literacy is a tool of development and eradication of illiteracy is important both for the conquest of poverty and for healthy functioning of the government system. Efforts should be made to cover the entire illiterate population of the age-group 15–35 under the adult education programme by 1990" (Ministry of Education, 1985).

In this endeavour, the adult education instructor has to play a crucial role in creating the necessary climate in the community so that the poor and the oppressed people can have confidence and self-reliance to stand on their own legs. The task of an adult education instructor is not only to teach literacy skills but also to bring about desirable changes in the behaviour of learners. According to Torrence (1971) "the instructor has to be much more than just a teacher. He should be a source of inspiration and advice as well as a companion to each of the individuals who come under his guidance. He needs an abundance of wisdom, tact and patience".

Malnutrition is widely prevalent in India. Nearly two-thirds of India's population is on a nutritionally deficient diet. Several surveys have shown that a large number of people eat less food than they need, the worst sufferers being pregnant women, lactating mothers and children. Malnutrition is not exclusively due to non-availability of nutritious food. Failure to use the available resource in a meaningful manner can be another cause. This is mainly due to lack of knowledge of the value of foods in relation to the needs of the individual. Ignorance and superstitions play a great role in the rejection of low-cost, locally available nutritious foods. The magnitude of malnutrition and the ignorance about the relationship of food to health among a majority of the population project the need for nutrition education and training at all levels. Nutrition education in a broad sense is a life long process, and it may bring about changes in knowledge, attitudes and practices in meeting individual and community needs. The predominant programme in vogue to provide such a knowledge to a large number of illiterates is the Adult Education Programme (AEP) or at present the National Literacy Mission (NLM). As a matter of fact this aspect of nutrition is incorporated in the curriculum of AEP. However, whether the instructors are properly equipped with the knowledge of nutrition, whether they possess favourable attitudes and right practices of nutrition is doubtful. Hence, the present study aims at identifying the existing levels of knowledge, attitudes and practices of nutrition among adult education instructors to develop their competence and to upgrade the technical know-how of the instructors for better instruction.

Statement of the Problem

> "*Knowledge, Attitudes and Practices of Nutrition Among Adult Education Programme Instructors in Andhra Pradesh*"

Need for the Study

The instructors are the backbone of the educational movement and the success of any development programme depends upon the attitude and involvement of the people by whom it is implemented. The instructor is not only the teacher of literacy but also the generator of awareness and disseminator of functional information. It means, the instructor has to create awareness about crucial national problems like poverty, malnutrition, population explosion, unemployment, illiteracy, etc., and provide functional knowledge. To do this job effectively, the instructor should have adequate knowledge, right attitude and practice of what he preaches so as to set a good example to be followed by others. The adult learners who attend adult education centres can be education by adult education instructors about the basic facts of nutrition in order to help remedy the nutritional problems. An enquiry into the existing levels of knowledge, attitudes and practices of the instructors in these areas would help to identify the gaps in the knowledge, attitudes and practices of instructor and to bridge the gaps by introducing relevant contents in the training programmes organised for them and also by producing and distributing among them suitable teaching, learning materials in these areas. Therefore, it is essential to assess the knowledge, attitudes and practices of nutrition among adult education instructors in Andhra Pradesh with a view to helping them to increase their functional competence. It is in this context that the present investigation was conceived.

Objectives of the Study

The main objectives of the study are :

1. to assess the levels of knowledge, attitudes and practices of nutrition among adult education programme instructors in Andhra Pradesh;
2. to suggest the probable items of nutrition that can be incorporated in the training programme course content of the adult education instructors on the basis of the gaps in knowledge, attitudes and practices;
3. to find out the influence of socio, economic and demographic factors on the knowledge, attitudes and practices of nutrition among adult education instructors;
4. to assess the inter-relationships among knowledge, attitudes and practices in nutrition of adult education insturctors;
5. to study the differential contribution of the socio, economic and demographic variables in predicting the knowledge, attitudes and practices of nutrition among adult education instructors.

Hypothesis

On the basis of the above objectives, the following hypotheses are formulated.

1. The levels of knowledge, attitudes and practices of nutrition among adult education instructors are inadequate.

2. There exists variations in the level of knowledge attitudes and practices on different items of nutrition among the adult education instructors.
3. There would not be any significant influence on socio, economic and demographic factors on the knowledge of nutrition among adult education instructors (Each one of the independent variables will be considered separately to test the hypothesis).
4. The influence of socio, economic and demographic factors on the attitude of adult education instructors towards nutrition would not to be significant (Each one of the independent variables will be considered separately to test the hypothesis).
5. The practices of nutrition among adult education instructors would not be significantly influenced by their socio, economic and demographic factors (Each one of the independent variables will be considered separately to test the hypothesis).
6. There exists a positive and significant inter-relationship between the knowledge, attitudes and practices of nutrition among adult education instructors.
7. The contribution of socio, economic and demographic variables in predicting the knowledge of nutrition among adult education instructors would not vary significantly.
8. There would not be any significant variation in the amount of contribution made by different socio, economic and demographic variables to the prediction of attitudes of adult education instructors toward nutrition.
9. The contribution of socio, economic and demographic variables in predicting the practices of nutrition among adult education instructors would not vary significantly.

The Variables

To carry out the investigation, apart from the three dependent variables viz., knowledge, attitudes and practices, the following independent variables are included in the study : (1) Age, (2) Sex, (3)

Annual income of the family, (4) Caste, (5) Religion, (6) Marital Status, (7) Occupation, (8) Educational Status, (9) Type of the family, (10) Size of the family, (11) Experience as an adult education instructor, (12) Reading Newspapers, (13) Listening to Radio, (14) Viewing Films, (15) Viewing Filmshows and (16) Viewing Television.

Brief Description of the Variables

The following definitions/descriptions are operationalized for the purpose of measuring the variables in the study.

Dependent Variables

i) Knowledge : Concepts in nutrition are not developed automatically by exposure. They come to be a part of one's thinking when the teacher guides the learner to see relationships between nutrition facts and his own experience. Any known, identified, and recognized nutrition problem is well worth solving. The investigator does not intend to disconnect the need for nutrition knowledge (facts, information) in using problem solving as a method of nutrition education. Without sound and current nutrition knowledge, problem solving would be a fake. Without problem solving nutrition knowledge per se may be meaningless, uninteresting and of little value to learners. The learner needs to become involved in the problem solving process before he is told "what and how much to eat" or even shown how to prepare nutritionally adequate food (Scrimshaw, 1969).

According to the concise Oxford Dictionary of Current English (1981) the word knowledge means "knowing, familiarity gained by experience (of person, thing, fact)".

Bloom (1956) defines knowledge as 'those behaviours and test situations which emphasize remembering them by recognition or recall of ideas, materials and phenomena.

Gronlund (1970) defines it as the remembering of previously learned material. This may involve the recall of a wide range of material, from specific facts to complete theories, but all that is required is the bringing to mind the appropriate information. Knowledge represents the lowest level of learning outcomes in the cognitive domain.

ii) Attitude : Success in nutrition education is expressed as the incorporation of sound nutritional knowledge into daily practice. Among the variables affecting both the acquisition of knowledge and its later application is the learners attitude.

Carruth et al (1977) quote, Summers as saying that attitudes have a motivational quality. Attitudes not only contribute to routinizing behaviour but they have a directional quality in that they involve an affective dimension, such as a person's evaluation of liking for or emotional response to the attitude object.

In the dictionary of philosophy and psychology, Baldwin (1905) defines attitude as "readiness for attention or action of a definite sort". Allport (1929) refers to treat attitude as 'a mental and neutral state of readiness, organised through experience, exerting a director or dynamic influence upon the individual's response to all objectives and situations with which it is related".

To Bogardus (1941) attitude is a tendency to act toward or against something in the environment which becomes thereby a positive or negative value. According to Morgan (1934), "attitudes are literally mental postures, guides, for conduct before a response is made". Warren (1934) defines attitude as a specific mental disposition toward an incoming (or arising) experience, whereby that experience is modified, or a condition of readiness for a certain type of activity".

Coleman (1975) describes attitudes as a consistent learned emotional predisposition to respond in a particular way to a given object, person or situation.

Thurstone (1947) defines an attitude as "the degree of positive or negative effect associated with some psychological object". An individual who associates a positive effect or feeling with some psychological object is said to like the object. An individual who has associated a negative effect with the same psychological object would be said to dislike that object or to have unfavourable attitude towards the object (Edwards, 1967).

Freeman (1962) describes attitude as "a dispositional readiness to respond for certain situations, persons or subjects in a constant manner which has been learned and has become one's typical mode of response".

All the definitions cited above give importance to the degree of 'liking' or 'disliking' towards a psychological object.

In this investigation, the word attitude refers to "a mental and neural state of readiness in his learning through experience, exerting a directive or dynamic influence upon the individual's responses to all subjects and situations with which it is related".

iii) Practices : It is the behavioural manifestation of the nutrition knowledge of an individual. Chaplin (1975) describes practice as the repetition of an act or behavioural function for the purpose of improving the function. Practice is that which is customary, typical and habitual. It is operationalised for the purpose of measuring various practices with regard to nutrition by considering different items of nutrition knowledge.

Independent Variables

(i) Age : As there exist contradictory research results in establishing the relationship between age and knowledge of nutrition, age and attitude towards nutrition and age and practices of nutrition, it is decided to include age as one of the variables in the present investigation. The chronological age reported by the subjects is considered for the purpose.

(ii) Sex : Instructors of both sexes are included in the study to find out whether there is any significant difference between men and women instructors in the level of their knowledge, attitude and practices of nutrition.

(iii) Annual Income of the Family : The total income of the instructor and also that of other members of the family from all sources is calculated. On the basis of this the instructors are divided into four categories and the significant differences between the level of knowledge, attitudes and practices of four groups are tested.

(iv) Caste : The sample of instructors is divided into three caste groups viz., those belonging to (1) forward caste, (2) backward caste, and (3) scheduled castes and scheduled tribes, based on the original caste mentioned by the respondent to see whether there exists any difference between the three groups.

(v) Religion : As there exist contradictory research results in establishing the relationship between religion and knowledge of nutrition, religion and attitude towards nutrition, and religion and practices of nutrition, it is decided to include religion as one of the variables in the present investigation. The religion mentioned by the respondents are considered for the purpose.

(vi) Marital status : The sample of instructors who participated in the study are divided into two groups on the basis of their marital status i.e., married and unmarried. The knowledge scores, attitude scores and practice scores of instructors are analysed to see whether there exists any significant difference between the two groups.

(vii) Occupation : All most all the instructors are employed in some profession or other and the instructor's position is only a part-time work for them. Therefore, it is defined as the occupation of the respondent or his family from which he/she is securing the highest income. Based on this the instructors are classified into four categories and their knowledge, attitude and practices scores are analysed.

(viii) Educational Status : As it is observed from the review of literature, that the level of education of instructors influences their level of knowledge, attitudes and practices of nutrition, it is decided to include the educational qualifications of the instructors as one of the variables in the present study. The instructors with minimum qualifications, i.e., 8 years of schooling are being treated as one group. The instructors possessing more qualifications than required are classified into three groups namely, those who have had 10 years of schooling, 12 years of schooling and above 12 years of schooling.

(ix) Type of the Family : The instructors who participated in the study are divided into two groups, viz., those who are from (1) joint family and (2) nuclear family. The joint family is one which is composed of two or more couples and their children including old persons related to them. The nuclear family is one which is composed of a husband, a wife and their unmarried children.

(x) Size of the Family : Family size of the instructors has been taken as another variables to see if it has any influence on the dependent variables. It is believed that those possessing more number of dependents or those who are from large families may be more frequently disturbed than others having less number of dependents or belonging to small families. Hence, the number of people in the family as reported by the respondent is considered as one of the variables in the study.

(xi) Experience : The number of years an individual has been working as instructor is considered as one of the variables in the study to see the effect of it on the three dependent variables, viz., knowledge, attitudes and practices of nutrition.

(xii) Mass Media Exposure : It is a direct exposure of the respondents to Newspapers, Radio, Movies, Film shows and Television. It was observed in the review of past research that the relationship between mass media exposure and (1) knowledge, (2) attitudes, and (3) practices was complex and contradictory. Hence, mass media exposure is considered as one of the variables in the present study.

Definition of Certain Terms and Concepts Used

(i) Nutrition : The word nutrition is derived from the 'nutricus' meaning "to suckle at the breast".

According to the Pocket Medical Dictionary by Nancy Roper (1970) the word nutrition means "the sum total of the processes by which the living organism receives and utilizes the materials necessary for survival, growth and repair of worn out tissues".

Nutrition may be defined as a science concerned with the production, intake, function, balance and health effects of chemical materials that provide nourishment (Review of Nutrition and Food Science, 1970).

According to Magnus Pyke (1961), nutrition is the science that deals with the study of all the processes concerned in the growth, maintenance and repair of the living body which are connected in a fairly direct way the nutrients supplied by food.

Nutrition is the science of nourishment, including the study of the nutrients that each organism must obtain from its environment in order to maintain life and reproduce (Food, Agriculture and Nutrition — Roger J. Williams, 1964).

(ii) Malnutrition : Malnutrition is a state in which there is a deficiency in one or more of the essential metabolites necessary for maintenance and growth of the intact organism (Food, Agriculture and Nutrition—Donald W. King, 1977).

Malnutrition is the disturbance of form of function arising from a deficiency or excess of one or more nutrients (Dictionary of

Nutrition & Food Technology, Arnold E. Bender, 1982).

Malnutrition is an impairment of health from a deficiency, excess or imbalance of nutrients. It includes undernutrition.

(iii) Over-nutrition : An excess of one or more nutrients and usually of calories (Dictionary of Dietetics, Rhoda Ellis, 1956).

(iv) Undernutrition : A deficiency of calories and/or one or more essential nutrients.

Undernutrition is the change in structure of function of the cells owing to lack of one or more nutrients (Dictionary of Dietetics, Rhoda Ellis, 1956).

(v) Good Nutrition : The essential nutrients in correct amounts and balance are utilized to promote the highest level of physical and mental health throughout the entire life cycle.

(vi) AEP : AEP is the shortened form for Adult Education Programme which was launched on 2nd October 1978 by the Government of India.

(vi) Adult Education : The term 'Adult Education' includes all aspects of education of persons beyond the age of fourteen years. The scope of Adult Education is very vast for "being, becoming, belonging".

Liveright and Haygood (1969) proposed that "adult education is the process whereby persons who no longer (or did not) attend school on a regular and full time basis undertake sequential and organised activities with a conscious intention of bringing about changes in information, knowledge, understanding skills, appreciation and attitudes, or for the purpose of identifying and solving personal or community problems".

Bertelsen's (1974) definition is simply that "adult education is any learning experience designed for adults irrespective of content, level and methods used.......".

The term 'adult education' is defined by UNESCO as the entire body of organised educational process; whatever the content, level and method, whether formal or otherwise, whether they prolong or replace initial education in schools, colleges and universities as well as in apprenticeship, whereby persons regarded as adult by the society to which they belong, develop their abilities, enrich their knowledge, improve their technical or professional qualifications and bring about changes in their attitude or behaviour in the two-fold perspective of full personal development and participation in balanced and independent social, economic and cultural development".

(viii) Instructor : Instructor is an educational agent providing supervision in an adult education setting.

Good in his Dictionary of Education provides the meaning for the term 'Instructor' as follows :

"He is an individual employed in an adult education programme who provides learning experiences for illiterate adults. He is a person with specialised training, education and/or significant professional experience in the field of adult education, involved in the planning and directing or educational activities for adults".

In the adult education programme, any man or woman who has studied upto the 8th class (in exceptional cases upto the 5th class), who has certain leadership qualities, who will be accepted by the community as a responsible person and who has desire to organise adult education centre is appointed as instructor. Instructors are those who are working as grass root level workers in the Adult Education Programme. The Instructor is the front-line worker in the adult education programme. He is the actual 'doer' of adult education in the community. The instructor has to play the following roles :

1. An organiser of the centre
2. Teacher of literacy
3. Generator of awareness
4. Disseminator of functional information
5. Mobilizer of resources
6. Leader, organiser of cultural and recreational programme
7. Recorder of the process of change and learning.
8. Manager of the centre

The quality and success of work in any centre depends upon the capacity and sincerity of the instructor.

Limitations of the Study

Owing to limitation of time, the study is restricted only (a) to nutritional knowledge, attitudes and practices leaving knowledge, attitude and practices in other areas like health, politics, law, etc., (b) it is limited only to the instructors of 1987–88 batch in Andhra Pradesh and the sample is restricted to 600 instructors only, and (c) only an adequate number of socio, economic and demographic variables that are supposed to possess an impact on the dependent variables alone could be included in the present study.

4

Methods of Investigation

This chapter deals with the various tools already available for measuring knowledge, attitudes and practices of nutrition, the various procedures employed in the construction and standardization of data gathering instruments on different variables included in the study, the methods adopted in selection of samples, collection of data and mode of scoring.

Out of the 19 variables (both dependent and independent) included in the study, 16 are personal and demographic variables, for which information was gathered through a personal data sheet. The remaining 3 were measured with suitable instruments. The three instruments, namely, knowledge test, attitude scale and practice check-list to measure knowledge, attitudes and practices were developed by the present investigator. The different techniques and procedures followed in the development of the instruments are discussed in the succeeding sections of this chapter.

Tools Already Available for Measuring Knowledge, Attitudes and Practices of Nutrition

It may not be out of place to describe briefly the instruments which were developed by earlier researchers to understand the implications of constructing a test or scale and to know the utility of such instruments in the present context. The tools available to measure knowledge, attitudes, and practices of nutrition are described below separately alongwith their utilitarian aspects.

Knowledge

Eppright et al., (1970) developed a knowledge test composed of 23 true/false items concerning the factual information on nutrition. By this test the score of nutritional knowledge could be obtained in terms of the total number of correct responses. Each respondent was also asked to answer oral questions in this regard. The principle behind the use of true/false items in the knowledge test was to enable the respondents to provide valid answers.

Schwartz (1975) revised the instrument of Eppright et al., (1970). The modified instrument provided two responses for each statement. The first response was to true/false type while the second was of 4-point continuum, viz., very confident to very doubtful.

McNutt (1977) criticized the methodologies that had been used to measure nutrition knowledge. He complained that most researchers tend to access the "recitation of the names of nutrients and their isolated functions rather than probing the individual's competency to select a diet appropriate to his or her nutritional needs". He provided few clear guidelines for nutrition educators who wish to modify people's food choice by providing them with nutrition information.

Dugdale et al., (1979) reported that nutritional knowledge could be obtained by scientific as well as non-scientific means. Misconceptions and fallacious opinions find a place if knowledge is tested by non-scientific means. Therefore, the scientific testing of levels and accuracy of the nutritional knowledge was essential.

Dugdale and his co-workers evolved an innovative methodology for assessment of nutritional knowledge. The simplest and most common questions were formulated. They preferred the question form to statement because it stimulates thinking about the ideas in the respondent. The correct level of knowledge was obtained by dividing the number of correct responses by the number of questions. If the respondent was given an additional alternative of 'do not know' to each of the questions much more information could be obtained. Through this alternative the respondent admitted that either he had no knowledge or was uncertain about the correct answer. Conversely, if the subject marked only the 'yes' or 'no' alternative, he believed that he had that knowledge. This knowledge could be designated as 'perceived' knowledge. The level of perceived knowledge could be obtained from the three alternative questionnaire by using the formula, viz., Perceived Knowledge = Number of questions marked yes/ no Total number of questions.

However, the fact that a person has an idea on a given subject is no guarantee that the idea is accurate. Such accuracy is obviously important and could be derived from the three alternative questionnaire as follows : Accuracy of Knowledge = Number of correct responses. Number of responses marked yes/no. These three aspects of knowledge are related to one another. Correct knowledge = Perceived knowledge × Accuracy of knowledge.

A high level of correct knowledge is the ultimate aim of nutrition educators. If the respondents' level of correct knowledge is unsatisfactory, the three alternative procedures enables the investigator to identify as to where the problem is ? This method of assessment of knowledge was tested by Dugdale et al., (1979) and found to be valid and reliable.

Olson and Sims (1980) maintained that an information processing approach provided a conceptual foundation for explaining the effects of peoples' nutrition knowledge on their food behaviour. This perspective focussed on the psychological processes involved in *acquiring* nutrition information, *storing* it in memory, *retrieving* it at a later time and *using* it in decision-making. Further, they suggested that multiple measures to be developed to organise peoples' nutritional knowledge structures. The reliability and validity of these indices must be established. Then it would be easy to examine how different types of knowledge structures were related to the use of new nutrition information for making correct-food choices. They concluded that the results of such research had the potential to help nutrition educators and policy makers, develop more effective nutrition education programmes.

Attitudes

Attitude has been described as an underlying disposition which enters, along with other influences, into the determination of a variety of behaviours towards an object (Cook and Sellitz, 1964). Attitude includes a *cognitive* component that reflects some *emotional feeling* connected with these beliefs and an *action tendency* that indicates a readiness to respond in a particular way (Freedman et al., 1974 and Kelly, 1977). A useful attitude scale must possess the properties of reliability, validity, unidimensionality, equality of units and a zero point (Shaw and Wright, 1967). Carruth and Anderson (1977) have suggested that without a more rigorous methodology, attitude measurement in nutrition education will remain at the descriptive level of research.

O'Connel et al., (1981) point out that assessment of an individual's attitude toward an object is a complex task. Instruments designed for the purpose may take into consideration any or all the three attitude components. Cook and Sellitz (1964) have argued that since different approaches used by researchers for estimation of attitudes may bring out different facets of the attitude component, researchers should not expect that data from these approaches will be perfectly correlated.

Eppright et al., (1970) developed a nutritional attitude test and validated it. It consisted of 30 items in all of which 11 items related to attitude toward nutrition and eating habits, 8 items about meal planning, and 11 items about food preparation.

Sims (1976) adopted the Parental Attitude Research Instrument (PARI) of Schaefer and Bell (1958). The extent of agreement or disagreement was scored on a Likert-type format using a 4-point continuum. Out of ten, only four variables were chosen which showed important relationship to nutritional knowledge. They were 'Nutrition is important', 'Equalitarian', 'Parents are all wise' and 'Powerlessness'. In all, high reliability (ranging from 0.71 to 0.79) and validity were established.

Carruth and Anderson (1977) developed a scale to measure attitude towards food and nutrition. A pool of statements that fulfilled scaling criteria—validity, reliability, unidimensionality and rigidity—flexibility were identified. Content validity was established based on the 75 per cent or more of expert opinion. Through this process, sixty items were selected from the original pool of 128. The degree of rigidity and flexibility was judged by the experts using the eleven-point continuum, median of distribution (S values) and interquartile range (Q values), and finally 40 statements were chosen for the final version of the attitude instrument. Likert type format of 5-point continuum—strongly agree to strongly disagree, was found to be suitable. Unidimensionality was established using factor analysis.

Reliability was established using test-retest method.

A few explorations have shown the value of applying the semantic differential to nutritional attitude assessment (Brinton, 1961; Shaw and Wright, 1967).

Carruth and Musgrave (1979) developed a semantic differential instrument to assess attitude change toward community nutrition. A semantic differential means' pairs of adjectives rather than words in the context of a sentence or phrase, to which a person responds. It was designated to measure individual reactions to semantic objects utilizing ratings of bipolar adjectives called scales. The adjective pairs included were such a flexible-rigid, good-bad, slow-fast, etc. The semantic differential was utilized to measure the inter-relationships among four attitude variables in teacher evaluation and was found to be an effective method. The attitude variables measured were credibility, content, delivery and feedback (McDowell, 1975). The semantic differential has been recommended as a means of assessing students' affective behaviour because it possesses a great deal of flexibility, easy to construct and simple to score.

Rajyalakshmi et al., (1980) attempted to develop an attitude scale to measure attitudes of rural women towards food and nutrition. The method of scalogram analysis (Edward, 1957) was followed in constructing the instrument to measure the attitudes. Collection of items was done consulting various sources. An item pool containing 120 items was prepared. The items were edited by following the criteria suggested by Edward (1957). Thus a set of 55 items were classified according to their content under different relevant sub-concepts such as cereals and millets, legumes and oil seeds, etc. The number of items under each concept ranged from 2 to 9.

The items were administered to 100 rural women of the Telengana region, Andhra Pradesh. Five-point continuum ranged from strongly agree (4) to strongly disagree (0) for the favourable items. For unfavourable attitude items, the scoring system was reversed i.e., 0–4.

Reliability and scalability of the instrument were tested using the Coefficient of Reproducibility (CR) and Minimum Marginal Coefficient of Reproducibility (MMCR) respectively.

The following formulae were used to calculate CR and MMCR:

$$CR = 1 - \frac{\text{Total number of errors}}{\text{No. of respondents} \times \text{No. of items}}$$

$$MMCR = \frac{\text{Sum of Responses}}{\text{No. of items}}$$

Modifications were made in each category by making different combinations of items. As a result, the number of items in the scale was reduced from 55 to 44 and the number of items under each sub-concept ranged from 2 to 7. Since the CR values for all the categories were above 0.80, all the items were reliable. Whereas the MMCR values were above 6.5, all the items were scalable. Validation of the instrument was established by the Jury. Sample items were : (1) Hand pound rice is better than milled rice, (2) Thorough washing of rice before cooking is good.

Sutnick (1981) examined the use of 'Q' sort technique in attitude assessment. The study was conducted among the students of Intermediate unit in Luzerne country. It was reported that the food 'Q' sort consisted of sets of 25 cards with names of foods. These foods were divided into 4 categories based on their nutritive values : high, moderate, somewhat and least. Respondents were asked to sort the foods along 2 dimensions—preference and nutritive value. The accuracy of the nutritive value sequence was taken as a measure of the respondents' knowledge. It was assumed that attitudes toward good selection would be truly reflected in their preference rankings. If the students were motivated to value nutrition more highly in making food choices, this would be observed as a more positive correlation between the two ratings. Thus, the method identified nutritional attitudes. After testing 'Q' sort technique the author stated that this technique could be of great value to the nutrition educators.

Practices

Pelto (1981) reported that the method of participant observation was articulated by Malinowski in 1961. This method having been modified by many researchers has come to be a usable form. This technique facilitates systematic exploration of relationships among events through interviewing, meticulous eye witness and administering tests. Thus the method has been converted to scientific use.

Schwartz (1975) suggested a procedure with two dimensions for assessing nutritional practices. The two dimensions were :

1. Dietary intake was assessed based on frequency of intake during a 3-day period.
2. Descriptive statements indicative of observable nutritional practices such as use of supplements, etc. were used. These items could also be quantified as in the case of knowledge test.

Carruth et al., (1977) documented three types of nutritional related behaviours in their study. They were :

1. Requests for free literature from the respondents,
2. Verbal affirmations of nutritional practices from the respondents. An example of verbal behaviour would be "respondent recommending the basic 4 food groups as a basis for menu planning",
3. Observed overt nutritional behaviours of respondents. An example of overt behaviour would be "a respondent eating a meal that contained foods selected from atleast three of the four food groups".

A check-list for both verbal and overt behaviours was developed.

Observations were not recorded in the presence of the participants. A disguised participant-observer design was used to document nutritional behaviours. A second observer assisted in cross-validating observations of both verbal and overt applications of nutritional knowledge.

Pelto (1981) stated that participant observation could be directed to include both process (formative) and product (outcome) evaluation.

Though there are a number of tools already developed to find out the knowledge, attitudes and practices of rural women, students, teachers, administrators, etc. towards nutrition, none of them is suitable for measuring the knowledge, attitudes and practices of adult education programme instructors towards nutrition as to tools were not developed by following usual psychometric methods. Moreover, most of the instruments referred to above were developed to suit the needs of foreign countries. The conditions prevailing in our country are entirely different and thereby it is felt that a separate instrument should be developed for the present purpose. Another reason for the present investigator to resort to develop her own instruments is to have a common base (same items) for measuring knowledge, attitudes and practices of nutrition. The above reasons made the investigator to construct a test following the psychometric procedures.

Development of Instruments

Three instruments were prepared for the measurement of knowledge, attitudes and practices of nutrition among adult education programme instructors.

Construction of Knowledge Test to Measure Knowledge in Nutrition

As nutrition comprises of many areas, it became necessary for the investigator to identify the areas that could be included in the test to be constructed along with the items under each area. On examination of the core content of nutrition, the investigator arrived at the following areas, namely, (i) Food and its importance, (ii) Food groups, (iii) Diet for pregnant and lactating mothers, (iv) Diet for infants, (v) Diet for pre-school children, (vi) Nutritional deficiency diseases, (vi) Cooking methods and their values, and (viii) Food-storage methods. These areas had also been authenticated by the experts working in the fields of nutrition education and adult education as the possible areas from which items could be developed for the test. Hence, the investigator finally decided to include these areas only, in the test to be developed.

The Item Pool

In constructing the test the investigator had to prepare test items in the Telugu language as it was planned to administer the test to the adult education programme (AEP) instructors in the State of Andhra Pradesh. To develop the test items the investigator made a thorough review of the related literature, consulted experts and the test items that had been used in various testing situations in India and elsewhere. Thus, a draft pool of items for the test was developed. These items were developed in such a way that they were not only more in number than required for the final test but also they were clear, concise and free from ambiguity. These draft items were given to some project officers, supervisors and also to a forum of AEP instructors in Puttur project of Andhra Pradesh with a request to point out any ambiguity, repetition and inaccuracy in them. At this stage, there were about 123 items in the test. Based on their suggestions all these test items were edited and reviewed. As a result of the rigorous culling out procedure only 63 items were retained. some of these items are given with two alternative responses (yes/no) and the majority of them are supplied with four alternatives (Multiple choice).

Try Out of the Items

The pilot form thus developed was administered to a random sample of 370 AEP Instructors selected from Kodur project of Cuddapah district (Rayalaseema area), Gadwal project of Mahaboobnagar district (Telengana area), Gudur project of Nellore district (Circars area).

The sample of 370 instructors for the pilot study were selected from among the AEP Instructors during 1986–87 by using a three-stage proportionate random sampling procedure. The details of the sampling procedure for the pilot study are given in Table 4.1.

Table 4.1 : Sample Selection Procedure for Try-out of the Tests and Scales

Regions	*Rayala-seema*	*Coastal Andhra*	*Telen-gana*	*Total*
Total Districts	4	9	10	23
I Stage				
Selection of Districts (by proportionate random sampling)	1	2	2	5
Total Projects	2	4	4	10
II Stage				
Selection of Projects (by proportionate random sampling)	1	2	2	5
Total Instructors	300	600	600	1,500
III Stage				
Selection of Instructors (by proportionate random sampling)	70	150	150	370

The respondents were requested to indicate the correct answer according to them by putting a "tick" " ✓ " mark against the answer. The data was collected by the investigator personally when the instructor came for monthly meetings.

Scoring

In scoring the test, a credit of one mark for the correct answer and zero for the wrong answer was given. The minimum and maximum scores on the test were 0 and 88. This was due to the presence of a few compound items containing two to three sub-items within themselves.

Item Analysis

The protocols scored for the knowledge test were arranged in the descending order of the total score of the test. Then the top 27 per cent (high group i.e., 100 respondents) and the bottom 27 per cent (low group i.e., 100 respondents) protocols were used to find out the item difficulty and item-discrimination power of each item. For each item of the knowledge test, the item difficulty (average of the two) and the discrimination index were calculated as per the procedure explained by Gronlund (1968).

For the purpose of illustration, the procedure employed for calculating difficulty level and discrimination power of an item is presented below :

Illustration

Item 2

Group	High Group (N = 100)	Low Group (N = 100)
Number of correct responses	83	34

Difficulty Level of the Item $\frac{83 + 34}{100 + 100} \times 100 = 58.5\%$

Note : *Since the difficulty level refers to the percentage getting the item right, the smaller the percentage figure the more difficulty the item.*

Discrimination Index of the Item $= \frac{83-34}{100} = 0.49$

An item that had a difficulty index between 35–85 per cent and a discriminating index of 0.20 or more were selected to be included in the final test.

Reliability of the Knowledge Test

The coefficient of reliability and validity for the knowledge test have been established on a random sample of 100 selected from Kodur project of Cuddapah district (Rayalaseema area), Gadwal project of Mahaboobnagar district (Telangana area), and Gudur project of Nellore district (Circars area). These 100 protocols have been selected randomly (using random numbers). Although, there are four different methods of estimating the reliability coefficient for a test, viz., (1) Test-retest method, (2) Parallel forms method, (3) The split-half method, and (4) The method of 'Rational Equivalence'. The split-half reliability method was employed in this case as it appeared to be most appropriate. The half-test reliability coefficient calculated on the basis of the 'odd-even' items was found to be 0.73 (vide Table 4.2). The reliability coefficient for whole test was estimated by employing the 'Spearman-Brown prophacy formula' and the value thus calculated was 0.84. As the coefficient is very high it may be said that the

Table 4.2 : Scattergram of Scores on 'Odd' and 'Even' Numbered Items

'Odd-items Scores' (Y-variable)		'Even-items Scores' (X-Variable)				fy
		10–14	15–19	20–24	25–29	
	10–14	5	1			6
	15–19	14	28	1		43
	20–24	1	10	30		41
	25–29		1	8	1	10
	fx	20	40	39	1	N = 100

$fy' = 55 \qquad fx' = 21$

$fy'^2 = 87 \qquad fx'^2 = 63$

$fy'x' = 54 \qquad N = 100$

$$r_{\frac{1}{2}\frac{1}{2}} = 0.73$$

Reliability for full test $= r_{11} = \dfrac{2\, r_{\frac{1}{2}\frac{1}{2}}}{1 + r_{\frac{1}{2}\frac{1}{2}}}$ (Spearman-Brown Prophacy formula)

i.e., $r_{11} = \dfrac{2 \times 0.73}{1 + 0.73} = 0.84$

test is a reliable tool for measuring the knowledge of nutrition among adult education instructors.

Validity of the Knowledge Test

The knowledge test does possess face validity, content validity, item validity, and intrinsic validity as it has been established. The details of each of these are given below.

(a) Face Validity

When the test was shown to few lay persons (adult learners in adult education centres), who had no knowledge of nutrition, they felt that it measured the knowledge of nutrition. Lindquist (1966) says, "a test is face valid particularly if it looks valid to layman" and therefore the test has face validity.

(b) Content Validity

Content validity indicates how adequate is the content of a test sampling the domain of which inferences are to be made. It is particularly important for achievement tests. To restore this type of validity to the test, an attempt was made to see that all the areas of nutrition were included in the test constructed. Under each area an adequate number of sample items were included. The preparation of test items was preceded by a thorough and systematic examination of all the areas of nutrition in books and journals. Experts were also consulted. The test items were reviewed in the light of the suggestions of the experts for content adequacy and accuracy. In view of these, it may be said that the test possesses content validity.

(c) Item Validity

The items of the knowledge test were selected on the basis of item analysis. Each item selected and included in the final test had a satisfactory level of item difficulty and item discrimination. Hence, the items included in the test possess item validity.

(d) Intrinsic Validity

The degree to which a test measures what it measures may be called its intrinsic validity. This definition can also be stated in terms of how well the obtained scores measure the test's true-score components. The validity is indicated by the square root of the proportion of true variance, in other words, the square root of its reliability. Another name for this statistic is the index of reliability (Guilford, 1954). The intrinsic value of the test was 0.84 = 0.9165 which indicates that the test possesses high intrinsic validity.

Development of Attitude Scale to Measure Attitudes Toward Nutrition

Methods of Measuring Attitudes

Thurstone defines an attitude as "the degree of positive or negative effect associated with some psychological object". By a psychological object, Thurston means by symbol, phrase, slogan, person, institution, ideal or idea towards which people can differ with respect to positive or negative effect (Edwards, 1969). Attitudes may be measured by a variety of methods and techniques of which direct questioning, projective tests, interviews, direct observation, questionnaire and attitude scales are some. The methods of direct questioning and interviews involve a lot of time and are most difficult to employ successfully. In measuring the attitudes the projective techniques suffer from certain disadvantages like difficulty in administering, scoring, reliability, etc. In the case of direct observation, it is difficult to have standardized and objective observation, since whatever the observer sees is entirely upto him and it involves the observer's personal likes and dislikes. Because of the above limitations of different methods and techniques, the questionnaire method is more popularly used.

In the questionnaire method, the individual is asked to express his/her opinion to the statements which are given in the form. The only means of inferring or estimating a person's in response to the statements in the questionnaire. This method of assessing attitude from expressed opinion is also subject to some limitations as the respondent tends to give socially acceptable responses thereby concealing his real attitude. But, this could be overcome in many ways such as making the questionnaire anonymous, etc.

Measurement and description of opinions and attitudes is an interesting are of research where data is collected in the form of expressed opinion of individuals. To obtain the measure of the attitude or belief of an individual or a group of individuals towards some phenomenon the inquiry form called opinionnaire or attitude scale is used.

Among the techniques available for the construction of attitude scales, mention could be made of the Thurstone Technique of Scaled Values, Thurstone's Method of Paired Comparisons, Likert's Method of Summated Ratings, Guttman's Scalogram Analysis or Method of Cumulating Scaling and Sherif's Social Judgement—Ego Involvement Approach. Among them are two popular and useful methods of measuring attitudes indirectly, commonly, used for research purposes and they are :

1) Thurstone Technique of Scaled Values
2) Likert Method of Summated Ratings.

Both the methods necessitate an initial collection of a large number of statements pertaining to an attitude object and of editing them. Thereafter, the methodology of the two techniques diverges. In the Thurstone technique which is based upon the psycho-physical method of equal appearing intervals—the scaling of the test items take place before the collection of data. Hence it is supposed to have a "rational baseline" and is said to be characterized by a "priori" approach. The Likert technique uses scaled responses and assumes that the final score is an average estimate that is obtained by the application of a number of different yardsticks (statements) each one of which extends to the whole length of the attitude continuum. This is in contrast to the Thurstone technique in which each item represents a specific part of the attitude continuum. The Likert technique is said to be characterised by an "aposterior" approach with an "empirical baseline".

Each technique has some advantages over the other. While the Thurstone technique makes use of objective judgements in the selection of items, it requires a large number of items to start with and a sizeable group of judges to rate the scale-value of the statements. The individual judgement by experts and computation of scale-value through the gives drawn on the placement of each statement by all the judges involves a laborious procedure. The Likert technique obviates these difficulties. While it dispenses with the judging group, it necessitates the psychometric methods of term-analysis (the internal consistency method or the correlation of individual items with the total score) which again is time consuming. It also involves a pretest by administering the items to a group of subjects representative of those with whom the scale is to be used. But the decided advantage of the Likert technique is its scope for the expression of intensity of an opinion through scaled responses. Further, the technique is believed to be easier and simpler in respect of construction. This scale is perceived to be relatively more reliable and valid, better understood and easy to fill-in (Shukla, 1972). The time required to construct this type of attitude scale is claimed to be less. Likert's technique is claimed to be more empirical (Nunnally, 1959). It is also claimed to be slightly more reliable than Thurston's (Krech and Crutch, 1948). This scale is claimed to provide more information about the subject's attitudes, since responses would be given to each of the many items (Adams, 1964). Moreover, the items in a Likert scale can be made to serve a dual function, to provide data on individual's opinions and attitudes about the specific issues covered by the single item as well as the total scale on the attitude or opinion dimension being studied. The Thurston items cannot secure the double function. For the reasons given above, the attitude scale constructed to measure the attitudes of Adult Education Programme Instructors towards nutrition was based on the Likert's technique.

The Item Pool

The first step in developing the scale was to collect a set of statements in such a way that the acceptance or rejection of each one would imply a different degree of favourable or unfavourable attitude towards nutrition. For this, a large number of statements on each aspect of nutrition were collected from various sources such as relevant literature, experts in the field and the opinion of the instructors, supervisors and project officers of the adult education programme. A few appropriate items in other scales were also taken. The different aspects of nutrition considered in collecting the items are (1) food and its importance, (2) food groups, (3) diet for pregnant and lactating mothers, (4) diet for infants, (5) diet for pre-school children, (6) nutritional deficiency diseases, (7) cooking methods and their values and (8) food-storage methods, However, all the items were drafted in such a way that the specific aspect on which the item was developed resembled the content aspect of knowledge items. Thus, the total number of items collected were 123.

Editing of Items

The editing process is very important in the Likert technique as there is no objective check on the ambiguity of the statements, analogues to the quartile deviation in the Thurston Method. These statements were shown to five experts and they were requested to screen them and suggest modifications, deletions and also to examine the statement for content accuracy, ambiguity and repetitions. The experts suggested elimination of a few statements which were ambiguous and the modification of a few other statements. After effecting changes based on their suggestions, the statements were reviewed and edited by the investigator in accordance with the guidelines suggested by Wang (1932), Thurstone and Chave (1929), Likert (1932), Bird (1940) and Edwards and Kilpatrick (1948) (Edwards, 1969). The following criteria suggested by Edwards and others were adhered to in editing the items :

a) The statements should be clear, short and simple;

b) The statement should be so worded that they can be endorsed or rejected;

c) Statements that are factual or capable of being interpreted as factual should be avoided;

d) Statements which are irrelevant to the attitude variable to be measured should be avoided;

e) Double barreled statement should be avoided;

f) Each statement should contain only one complete thought; and

g) Statements containing universal such as all, always, none and never, which often introduce ambiguity should be avoided.

After elimination of items which did not fulfil the above criteria, out of an initial collection of 123 items, 63 statements were retained on which a few items were compound in nature containing two to three sub-items with the same serial number. Thus, in total, 88 statements were finalized of which 45 were positive (favourable) and 43 were negative (unfavourable). These statements represented different shades of favourable and unfavourable attitudes towards the issue.

Against each statement three alternative responses, namely, Agree (A), Uncertain (U), and Disagree (DA) were given. The statements were then cyclostyled along with the standard directions and administered to 30 adult education programme instructors selected at random from the Puttur project mainly to know whether these statements could be easily understood by the instructors. From this preliminary try-out, it became known that the instructors could easily understand the statements and readily respond to them.

Try-out of Attitude Scale

The attitude scale thus prepared was administered to a random sample of 370 adult education programme instructors.

The sample of 370 respondents were selected based on a three-stage proportionate random sampling procedure which has already been explained while discussing the sampling procedure for the try-out of items of the knowledge test. Before the attitude scale was administered, instructions were read out loudly to the respondents and they were asked to read each of the statements carefully and to indicate their agreement or disagreement as per the category of responses given. The respondents were asked to put a "tick" mark against each statement in the appropriate parenthesis of the protocol of a respondent. The data was collected by the investigator personally when the instructors came for the monthly meetings.

Scoring of the Statements

The statements were scored in accordance with the general practice by assigning the following numerical weights to the positive and negative statements as shown below :

	Scoring Method		
	Agree (A)	Uncertain (U)	Disagree (DA)
Positive or favourable items	3	2	1
Negative or unfavourable items	1	2	3

The score of each respondents were computed by summing the weights of the responses made to each individual item. The range of the total score on the scale under the present scoring system is 88–264.

Item Analysis

As the try-out was conducted on 370 instructors, a group of 100 respondents (27 per cent) with the highest scores constituted the high group and a group of 100 (27 per cent) respondents with the lowest total scores formed the low group. These two groups were selected to be the criterion groups for calculating the critical ratio for each item. Sample size in the present study being 370, frequency in high group 100 (XH) and frequency in the low group 100 (XL) were equal and therefore, the critical ratio was calculated by following the formula suggested by Edwards (1969). The 't' values calculated for each item gave the discriminating index of each item.

$$t = \frac{\overline{X}_H - \overline{X}_L}{\sqrt{\frac{(XH - \overline{X}H)^2 + (XL - \overline{X}L)^2}{n(n-1)}}}$$

where

$$(XH - \overline{X}H)^2 = X^2H - \frac{(XH)^2}{n}$$

$$(XL - \overline{X}L)^2 = X^2L - \frac{(XL)^2}{n}$$

X^2H = Sum of the scores of the individual scores in the high group

X^2L = Sum of the scores of the individual scores in the low group

$\overline{X}H$ = The mean score of a give statement for the high group

$\overline{X}L$ = The mean score of a given statement for the low group

n = Number of respondents in each group

Application of this formula is illustrated with reference to the data pertaining to item number 2 of the attitude scale on nutrition.

The 't' values were similarly calculated for all the items used in the pilot study.

As suggested by Edwards (1957), the Thumb rule of rejecting items with 't' value of less than 1.75 was followed. Based on this

Table 4.3 : Calculation of Critical Ratio

Response Categories	High Group x	f	fx	fx^2	Low Group x	f	fx	fx^2
Agree	3	57	171	513	3	28	84	252
Uncertain	2	25	50	100	2	23	46	92
Disagree	1	18	18	18	1	49	49	49
		100	239	631		100	179	393
		nH	XH	X^2H		nL	XL	X^2L

$$\overline{X}H = \frac{239}{100} = 2.39 \qquad \overline{X}L = \frac{179}{100} = 1.79$$

$$(XH-\overline{X}H)^2 = 631 - \frac{(239)^2}{100} = 631 - 571.21 = 59.79$$

$$(XL-\overline{X}L)^2 = 393 - \frac{(179)^2}{100} = 393 - 320.41 = 72.59$$

$$t = \frac{2.39 - 1.79}{\sqrt{\frac{59.79 + 72.59}{100(100-1)}}} = \frac{0.6}{\sqrt{\frac{132.28}{9900}}} = \frac{0.6}{\sqrt{0.01337}}$$

$$= \frac{0.6}{0.1156} = 5.9103$$

$$t = 5.9103$$

criterion items having 't' values equal or greater than 1.75 were included in the final scale. Although the calculated 't' value was acceptable, some of the items were deleted for want of uniformity in content area in the three tests, viz., knowledge test, attitude scale and practice check-list. Finally, only 35 items were retained in the attitude scale on nutrition.

Reliability of the Attitude Scale

The coefficients of the reliability and validity have been established on a random sample of 100, selected from Kodur project of Cuddapah district (Rayalaseema area), Gadwal project of Mahaboobnagar district (Telengana area), and Gudur project of Nellore district (Circars area). These 100 protocols have been drawn at random (using random numbers). As explained earlier, there are four different methods of estimating the reliability of a scale. In this case the split-half method of estimating reliability appeared to be more appropriate. The coefficient of reliability for half test ($r_{½½}$) on the basis of 'odd and even' items was found to be 0.79. The reliability coefficient for full test (r_{11}) was estimated by employing the Spearman-Brown prophecy formula and the value obtained was 0.88 (vide Table 4.4). As this value is sufficiently high and satisfactory it may be concluded that the scale is possesses reliability.

Table 4.4 : Scattergram of Scores on 'Odd' and 'Even' Numbered Items

'Odd-items Scores' (Y-variable)	'Even-items Scores' (X-Variable)						fy
	75–79	80–84	85–89	90–94	95–99	100–104	
75–79	2	7	2				11
80–84	4	5	11				20
85–89		1	15	8	6		30
90–94			4	8	2	4	18
95–99				4	6	4	14
100–104					3	4	7
fx	6	13	32	20	17	12	N=100

fy'	= 25		fx'	= 65
fy'^2	= 201		fx'^2	= 233
$fy'x'$	= 169		N	= 100

$$r_{½½} = 0.79$$

Reliability for full test $= r_{11} = \frac{2\, r_{½½}}{1 + r_{½½}}$ (Spearman-Brown Prophacy formula)

i.e., $$r_{11} = \frac{2 \times 0.79}{1 + 0.79} = 0.88$$

Validity of the Attitude Scale

Four types of validity were established for the attitude scale. They are (1) Face validity, (2) Content validity, (3) Item validity and (4) Intrinsic validity.

a) Face Validity

The term face validity has many meanings and has been loosely used. It is best restricted to the fact that a test "looks" valid, particularly to those who are unsophisticated, in test practices. A more scientifically and professionally justifiable reason for face validity is to make it palatable to the examinee. If he feels that a test is relevant he is likely to have increased motivation in taking it, and uniformly high motivation is an important testing condition. When the scale was presented to the Readers and Professors of S.V. University conversant with test construction and when they were asked to express their opinion, they expressed that the test under construction looks valid and hence the scale has face validity.

(b) Content Validity

The related literature was consulted and an attempt was made to see that the items included in the scale were representative of all the areas of nutrition. The instrument was subjected to the scrutiny, criticism and comment of the experts in the field of adult education and nutrition. The scale was modified in the light of their comments and criticism. Thus it may be said that the scale possesses content validity.

c) Item Validity

Item validity emphasises the extent to which an item predicts segregation of examiners into those with high versus those with low criterion scores. The discriminating index was prepared for all the items and those items having high discriminating power (t = 1.75 or more) were retained in the final test. Hence, the scale has item validity.

d) Intrinsic Validity

As explained earlier, the intrinsic validity is given by the square root of the reliability of the instrument. Therefore, the intrinsic validity of the attitude scale was 0.88 = 0.9380.

Development of Check-list to Measure Nutritional Practices

For the measurement of nutritional practices a check-list was developed. The check-list consists of simple day to day observable practice items.

Item Pool

To develop the check-list items the investigator made a thorough review of the related literature, consulted experts on the test items that have been used in various testing situations in India and elsewhere. Thus, a draft pool of items for the test was developed in eight areas of nutrition already mentioned in development of knowledge test and attitude scale. these items were developed based on the knowledge items already prepared by the investigator. They were given to some project officers, supervisors and also to a forum of AEP Instructors with a request to point out any ambiguity, repetition, and inaccuracy in them. At this stage, there were about 85 items in the test. Based on the suggestions all these items were edited and reviewed. As a result of rigorous elimination procedure only 63 items were retained. Some of these items are placed with two alternative responses (yes/no) and the remaining are placed with four alternative responses (Multiple-choice).

Try-out of the Items

The items thus developed were administered on a random sample of 370 AEP instructors with necessary instructions. The sample of 370 respondents were selected based on a three-stage proportionate random sampling procedure which has already been explained while discussing the sampling procedure for the try-out of items of the knowledge test. Each item was supplied with alternative responses and the respondents were requested to mention the practices they are following by putting a "tick" mark against the response. The data was collected by the investigator personally. The responses thus given by the subjects were entered in their protocols.

Scoring

As the investigator would like to develop a test, the scoring pattern of the test was by using the answer key for the test. In scoring the test, a credit of one mark for the correct response and zero for the wrong response was given. The minimum and maximum score on the test were 0 and 63.

Item Analysis

The protocols scored for the practice test were arranged in the descending order of the total score of the test. Then the top 27 per cent (high group, i.e., 100 respondents) and the bottom 27 per cent (low group, i.e., 100 respondents) protocols were used to find out the item difficulty and item discrimination powers of each item. For each item of the practice test, the item difficulty (average of the two) and discrimination index were calculated as per the procedure explained in knowledge test.

Illustration

Item 2

Group	High Group (N = 100)	Low Group (N = 100)
Number of correct responses	83	44

$$\text{Item difficulty} \quad \frac{83 + 44}{100 + 100} \times 100 = 63.5\%$$

$$\text{Discrimination power of the Item} = \frac{83-44}{100} = 0.39$$

An item with a difficulty index between 30–80 per cent and a discriminating index of 0.20 per more was selected for inclusion in the final test. The final form of the check-list consists of 35 items.

Reliability of Practice Test

The coefficient of reliability and validity for the practice test have been established on a random sample of 100, selected from Kodur project of Cuddapah district (Rayalaseema area), Gadwal project of Mahaboobnagar district (Telengana area), and Gudur project of Nellore district (Circars area). These 100 respondents have been drawn randomly (using random numbers). As explained earlier, there are four different methods of estimating the reliability of a checklist. In this case, the Split-half method of estimating reliability appeared to be more appropriate. The coefficient of reliability for half test ($r_{½½}$) on the basis of 'odd and even' items was found to be 0.77. The reliability coefficient for full test (r_{11}) was estimated by employing the Spearman-Brown prophecy formula and the value obtained was 0.87 (Table 4.5). As this value is sufficiently high, it may be said that the check-list is a reliable tool.

Validity

As pointed out already, there are various methods of estimating the validity of a measuring instrument. The following types of validity

Table 4.5 : Scattergram of Scores on 'Odd' and 'Even' Numbered Items

'Odd-items Scores' (Y-variable)	'Even-items Scores' (X-Variable) 5–9	10–14	15–19	fy
5–9	8	1	9	
10–14	4	50	11	65
15–19		2	24	26
fx	12	53	35	N = 100

fy'	= 17	fx'	= 23
fy'^2	= 35	fx'^2	= 47
fy'x'	= 32	N	= 100

$$r_{\frac{1}{2}\frac{1}{2}} = 0.77$$

$$\text{Reliability for full test} = r_{11} = \frac{2\,r_{\frac{1}{2}\frac{1}{2}}}{1+r_{\frac{1}{2}\frac{1}{2}}} \quad \text{(Spearman-Brown Prophacy formula)}$$

$$\text{i.e.,} \quad r_{11} = \frac{2 \times 0.77}{1 + 0.77} = 0.87$$

were established for the practice check-list.

a) Face Validity

The check-list had face validity according to the opinion of adult education instructors and knowledgeable personnel in test construction. All of them expressed that the items appear to measure nutritional practices.

b) Content Validity

This form of validity is established by evaluating the relevance of the test items individually and as a whole. Each item should be a sampling of that aspect which the test purports to measure, and taken collectively, the items should constitute a representative sample of the variable that is measured. In the construction of the present instrument items were collected from the review of related literature, and from the comments of the experts in the field of nutrition and adult education. Thus, it can be reasonably assumed that the check-list has content validity.

c) Item Validity

There are numerous procedures by which item validity can be determined, one of which stresses the number of discriminations of the desired sort that the item is capable of making. It emphasises the extent to which the item predicts segregation of examinees into those with high versus low criterion scores. The discrimination power and difficulty level of each item were established, before including it into the final form. Hence, the items included in the final form of the test possess item validity.

d) Intrinsic Validity

Guilford (1954) defined intrinsic validity as 'the degree to which a test measures what it measures'. This can also be stated in terms of how well the obtained scores measure the test's true score component. This validity is given by the square root of its reliability. Hence, the intrinsic validity of the check-list was 0.87 = 0.9327.

Personal Data Sheet

The information with regard to age, sex, annual income of the family, caste, religion, marital status, occupation, educational status, type of the family, size of the family, experience as an adult education instructor, mass media exposure, etc., of the instructors was obtained from a carefully worded personal data sheet.

Locale of the Study

The locale of the study is the State of Andhra Pradesh in India. The State has three distinct regions, Rayalaseema, the Circars and Telengana. Rayalaseema is backward agriculturally, economically and socially. The Circars is the coastal region and it is agriculturally rich. Telengana is the most backward region agriculturally as well as economically in the State. Also it is linguistically more mixed than other regions and has a higher proportions of tribals.

The AEP was in operation in all the 23 districts of Andhra Pradesh during 1987–88. There were 46 projects in all the 23 districts of A.P. Out of these, 8 projects were located in Rayalaseema, 18 in the Circars and 20 in Telengana.

Sample Frame

The problem is aimed at investigating (finding out) the existing levels of knowledge, attitudes and practices of nutrition among adult education programme instructors in A.P. As the sample for the study has to be selected from a large population spread all over the State, a multistage random sampling technique was adopted. There were 46 projects in the 23 districts of A.P.

The State of Andhra Pradesh was first stratified according to the regions, viz., Rayalaseema, Coastal Andhra (Circars) and Telengana. As such, in the first stage, from each of the region two districts were selected at random, viz., Chittoor and Anantapur districts from Rayalaseema, Prakasam and Krishna districts from the Circars and Khammam and Warangal districts from Telengana. The number of projects in the selected districts were obtained from the District Adult Education Officers concerned.

In the second stage, one project from each of the selected districts was selected at random, thus making the total of projects included in the study six.

In the third stage, out of the 300 instructors in each project 100 were selected randomly. Thus a total of 600 adult education instructors working in six adult education projects of six districts of the three regions of Andhra Pradesh formed as the final sample for the present investigation.

(see detailed sample frame on p. 84)

Collection of Data

The necessary permission to collect data was obtained from the project officers (wherever data were collected). Through the project officers and assistant project officers, the supervisors were requested to make arrangements for the collection of data from the Instructors included in the sample. The adult education project has 10 sectors, each sector with 30 adult education instructors in charge of a supervisor. 10 adult education instructors from each sector were selected on random basis and this formed the sample of study from each project.

In order to gain confidence and to get their whole-hearted involvement in the investigation, the investigator established a good rapport with the instructors. The purpose of the study undertaken was made clear to the instructors and they were requested to give their answers to the schedules distributed to them when they attended a

The Detailed Sample Frame

Regions	*Rayala-seema*	*Circars*	*Telengana*	*Total*
Total districts	4	9	10	23
Total projects	8	18	20	46
I Stage				
Selection of the districts by random sampling	2	2	2	6
Total projects in the district	2+2	2+2	2+2	12
II Stage				
Selection of projects by random sampling	1+1	1+1	1+1	6
Total Adult Education Centres	300+300	300+300	300+300	1,800
III Stage				
Selection of Adult Education Centres by random sampling	100+100	100+100	100+100	600

monthly meeting. Every care was taken to make the respondents respond to the scales and tests without any hesitation on their part. The respondents were allowed to sit freely while responding. They were given adequate time to fill up the schedules. The doubts raised by them were cleared. Soon after administering the schedule, the duly filled in schedules were collected by the investigator after checking whether all the questions had been answered by the respondents.

Scoring

For scoring the knowledge test, attitude scale and practice check-list, the procedure followed in the pilot study was followed in the final study too.

The information provided by the respondents in the personal data sheet was also numerically coded to suit computer analysis.

Statistical Techniques Used

The total scores obtained by each of 600 adult education

instructors on all the variables were computed. The data were carefully analysed, appropriate statistical techniques like 't' test, 'F' ratio, Kramer's test, etc., were employed to know whether the independent variables could influence significantly the knowledge, attitudes and practices of nutrition among instructors.

The correlation coefficient (r) was computed to find out the inter-relationship between knowledge, attitudes and practices.

The simple correlation coefficient 'r' was computed between each one of the 16 independent variables and (1) knowledge, (2) attitudes and (3) practices of nutrition to identify the most significant variables associated with dependent variables. The multiple correlation coefficient 'R' was calculated by carrying out the step-wise regression analysis to find out the differential contribution of socio, economic and demographic variables in predicting the three dependent variables—knowledge, attitudes and practices. 't' test, 'F' ratio, Kramer's test, correlation coefficient (r), multiple correlation coefficient (R) and multiple regression were calculated by employing the usual procedures (Garrett, 1979; Kothari, 1986; Kramer, 1956). The next chapter deals with the analysis of the data in detail.

5

Analysis and Interpretation of Data

A systematic and step by step analysis of the data is presented under three sections as described below.

Section 1 : Descriptive Analysis

In this section, the analysis had been carried out on the basis of the responses made by the subjects to each one of the items so as to understand the level of knowledge and practices in each item of nutrition and the attitude towards each item of nutrition among adult education instructors. In other words, the item-wise analysis was carried on to identify the lapses of nutrition knowledge and practices and the unfavourable tendencies towards some of the specific nutrition aspects existing among the adult education instructors. The analysis was carried on by employing the percentages wherever necessary. Further, the distribution of scores on knowledge test, attitude scale and practice check-list are described. The descriptive statistics like measures of central tendency and measures of dispersion were calculated.

Section 2 : Influence of Independent Variables on Dependent Variables

This section deals with the study of the influence of socio, economic and demographic variables on the knowledge, attitudes and practices of nutrition. Various hypotheses formulated were tested by employing 't' test, 'F' test and Kramer's multiple range test appropriately.

Section 3 : Correlational Analysis

The simple coefficients of correlations were calculated for the three dependent variables, viz., knowledge, attitude and practices to know the inter-relationships among these variables. Further the multiple (step-wise) regression analysis was carried on and significant predictors of knowledge, attitudes and practices were identified along with the variance explained by them.

Section—1

Descriptive Analysis

The knowledge test and attitude scale has 35 questions and statements respectively. 12 questions/ statements have 2 sub-questions/statements (Sl. No. 4, 5, 9, 11, 13, 14, 22, 28, 30, 31, 33 and 35) and 2 questions/statements have 3 sub-questions/statements each (Sl. No. 17 and 20). Thus the knowledge test and attitude scale contains totally 51 items each. The practice check-list has 35 items.

Knowledge of Nutrition Among Adult Education Instructors

The total score on the entire knowledge test of 51 items describes the position of an individual's knowledge of nutrition. The mean score obtained by the sample of 600 respondents is 33.78. The median and mode are 34.36 and 35.52 respectively. The scores obtained by the sample varied from 13 to 49. Theoretically the score ranges from 0 to 51. Since the obtained mean is higher than half of the theoretically possible score, i.e., 25.5 (51/2 = 25.5), it can be concluded that the subjects in general are knowledgeable in nutrition. If we observe the frequencies shown in Table 5.1, it is seen that out of 600 subjects, 352 (58.66 per cent) scored above 25.5 and therefore, the respondents are possessing adequate knowledge.

The frequency distribution table of knowledge scores disclosed that the distribution is following normality. The skewness and kurtosis of the distribution are found to be –0.244 and 0.272 respectively. The values indicate that there is a little negative skewness in the distri-

Table 5.1 : The Frequency Distribution of Knowledge Scores of Nutrition

Class Interval	*Frequencies*	*Cumulative Frequencies*	*Smoothed Frequencies*
10–14	3	3	7
15–19	18	21	18
20–24	33	54	53.66
25–29	110	164	94.33
30–34	140	304	139.33
35–39	169	473	134.33
40–44	94	567	98.66
45–49	33	600	42.33

bution and it is slightly platykurtic (Fig. 5.1). The Standard Deviation (SD) of the distribution is 7.1229 with 13 as its minimum score and 49 as its maximum score. The range is 36 and the Quartile Deviation (QD) of the distribution is 4.9779 which is almost equal to 2/3 of SD. Thus the distribution of knowledge scores is following normality with slight divergencies.

Attitude Towards Nutrition Among Adult Education Instructors

It is not out of place to discuss about the different interpretation and meanings of neutral or zero point here to understand and interpret the results of the present investigation.

Attitudes are construed as varying in the quality and intensity (or strength) on a continuum from positive through neutral to negative (Krech et al., 1962; McGrath, 1964; Newcomb, Turner and Converse, 1965). The strength or intensity of the attitude is represented by the extremity of the position occupied on the continuum, becoming stronger as goes outward from a neutral position. But the neutral point of the attitude continuum poses a problem of interpretation, to which several alternative solutions have been proposed. First, one may consider the statement that an attitude is neutral to be self-contradictory, indicating the presence of a response predisposition on the one hand and the lack of a predisposition on the other. From this point of view, the neutral position on the attitude continuum represents no attitude towards the object in question (Shaw and Wright, 1967).

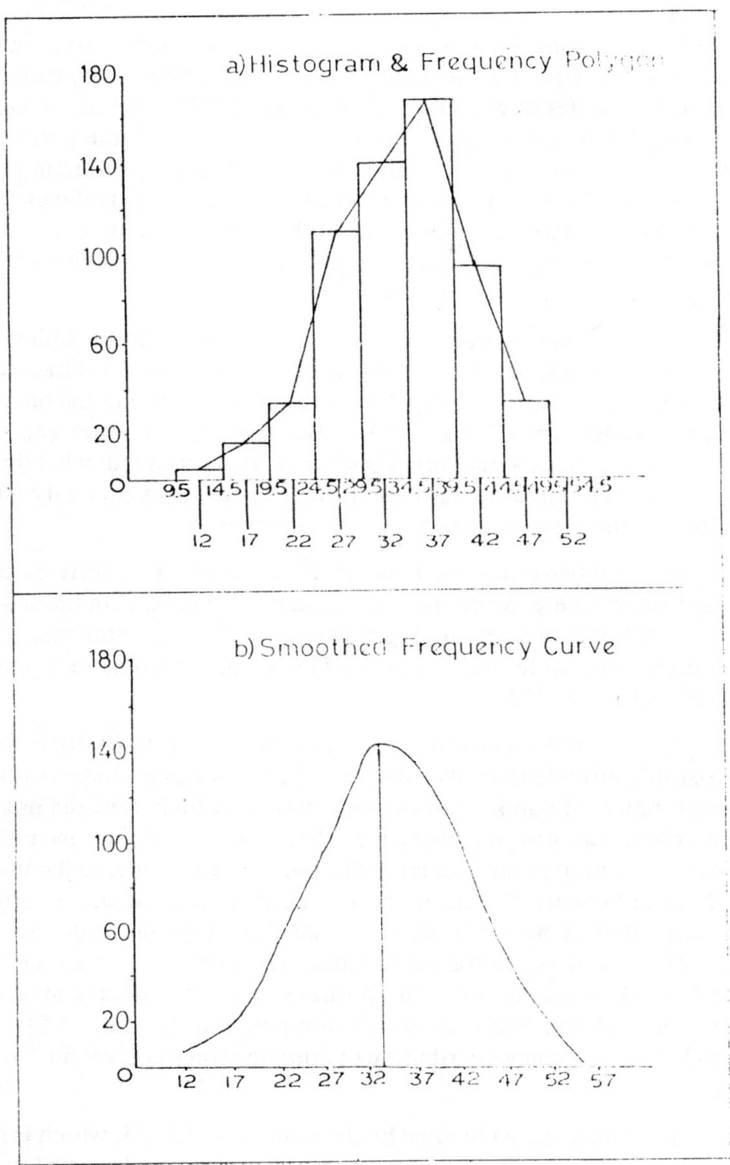

Fig. 5.1 : Distribution of Knowledge Scores

This interpretation supports the idea of Krech and Crutch Field (1948) that "attitudes always have either a positive or negative sign; if they have no sign (i.e., are neutral or at the zero point) they cannot be called attitudes at all..The second alternative interpretation suggested by Shaw and Wright (1967) is that it represents the point of balance in positive-negative evaluative conflict, thereby reflecting an ambivalent attitude, where ambivalence is used to indicate the existence of two or more attitudes toward the same refe-ent or several referents possessing some degree of similarity of stimulus value and being grouped as a referent class.

A third interpretation is based on neutral range scores achieved by inconsistent responses. It is that the subjects possessing such scores do not have integrated, clearly defined attitudes regarding the object under consideration (Walter, 1951). But this interpretation can be ignored as the instrument provides clear instructions about what they have to do. The investigator met all the respondents personally and motivated them properly to fill up the instrument.

The first two interpretations of the 'neutral point' or 'zero point' are considered here. Since the scale contains 15 items, with the score (or weight) on any item ranging between 1 and 3, the total score on the instrument could range between 51 and 153 with a neutral point of 102 (51 × 2 = 102).

A mean score above the neutral point indicates positive (or) favourable attitude towards nutrition. While a mean score below the neutral point, of course, shows unfavourable attitude towards nutrition. It is needless to point that a mean score of, say 103, just one point above the neutral point does not indicate definite attitude, as the little difference between the mean and neutral point may be due to error variance that is bound to occur in any investigation, more so in educational and psychological research. The total score on the entire scale of 51 items describes the position of an individual's attitude towards nutrition. The neutral (or) zero point on the scale is 51 × 2 = 102. The frequency distribution of attitude scores is given in Table 5.2.

The mean score obtained by the sample is 118.933, which is far above the neutral point. The obtained scores by the sample varied from 68 to 149. The values of median and mode are 119.54 and 120.754 respectively. The number of respondents whose score falls above and

Table 5.2 : The Frequency Distribution of Attitude Scores Towards Nutrition

Class Interval	*Frequencies*	*Cumulative Frequencies*	*Smoothed Frequencies*
65–74	5	5	3.66
75–84	6	11	11.66
85–94	24	35	33.33
95–104	70	105	74.66
105–114	130	235	109.66
115–124	129	364	130.00
125–134	131	495	116.33
135–144	89	584	78.66
145–154	16	600	35.00

below the neutral point is 515 (85.83 per cent) and 85 (14.17 per cent) respectively. Therefore, it can be concluded that the majority of the instructors under the study are having positive attitude towards nutrition. The standard deviation of the distribution of scores is 15.685 and the quartile deviation is 11.5516 which is slightly greater than 2/3 standard deviation. The skewness and kurtosis of the distribution are found to be –0.116 and 0.279 respectively. These values indicate that there is a little negative skewness in the distribution and it is slightly platykurtic (Fig. 5.2). Thus it is observed that the distribution follows normality with little exceptions.

Practice of Nutrition Among Adult Education Instructors

The practice check-list has 35 items. Theoretically the practice score of the individual varies from 0 to 35. The distribution of the practice scores obtained by the sample is shown Table 5.3.

The mean of distribution of the scores is 21.125. The median and mode are 21.15 and 21.20 respectively. The standard deviation of the distribution is 5.5924 and its Q.D. 3.7504 is almost equal to 2/3 S.D. The skewness and kurtosis are –0.013 and 0.270 respectively. The obtained score distribution has 0 as its minimum and 35 as its maximum. The range is 35. The distribution is slightly negatively skewed and it is slightly platykurtic (Fig. 5.3). But for the purpose of

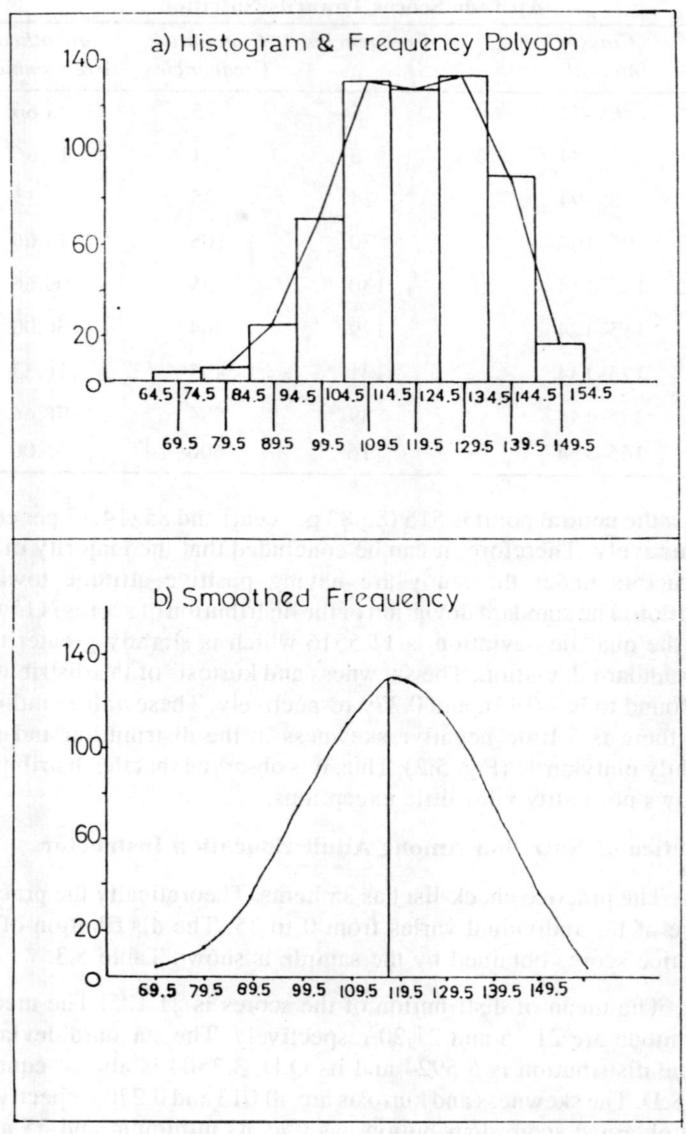

Fig. 5.2 : Distribution of Attitude Scores

Table 5.3 : The Frequency Distribution of Practice Scores of Nutrition

Class Interval	*Frequencies*	*Cumulative Frequencies*	*Smoothed Frequencies*
0–4	4	4	5
5–9	11	15	17.66
10–14	38	53	75.00
15–19	176	229	143.00
20–24	215	444	169.33
25–29	117	561	123.33
20–24	38	599	52.00
35–39	1	600	13.00

analysis it can be considered as normal distribution. Since the mean practice score obtained is higher than half of the theoretically possible score, i.e., 17.5 (35/2 = 17.5), it can be concluded that the adoption of nutritional practices is high among the adult education instructors. It is also supported by the fact that there are 464 respondents whose score is more than 17.5 and there are only 136 respondents whose score is below 17.5.

Thus the data presented show that the adult education instructors have adequate knowledge, favourable attitudes and adequate nutritional practices. Hence, the hypothesis that 'the levels of knowledge, attitudes and practices of nutrition among adult education instructors are inadequate', is rejected.

Item-wise Analysis of Knowledge, Attitude and Practice Scores

Though it is found, on the basis of total scores on knowledge, attitudes and practices, that adult education instructors have adequate knowledge, favourable attitude and adequate nutritional practices, further analysis is attempted to know whether there exists item-wise variations on knowledge, attitudes and practices and to identify the items on which the knowledge is high or low, the attitude is favourable or unfavourable and the practices are high or low.

The item-wise knowledge of instructors in terms of frequencies, percentages, proportions are shown in Table 5.4. A glance through

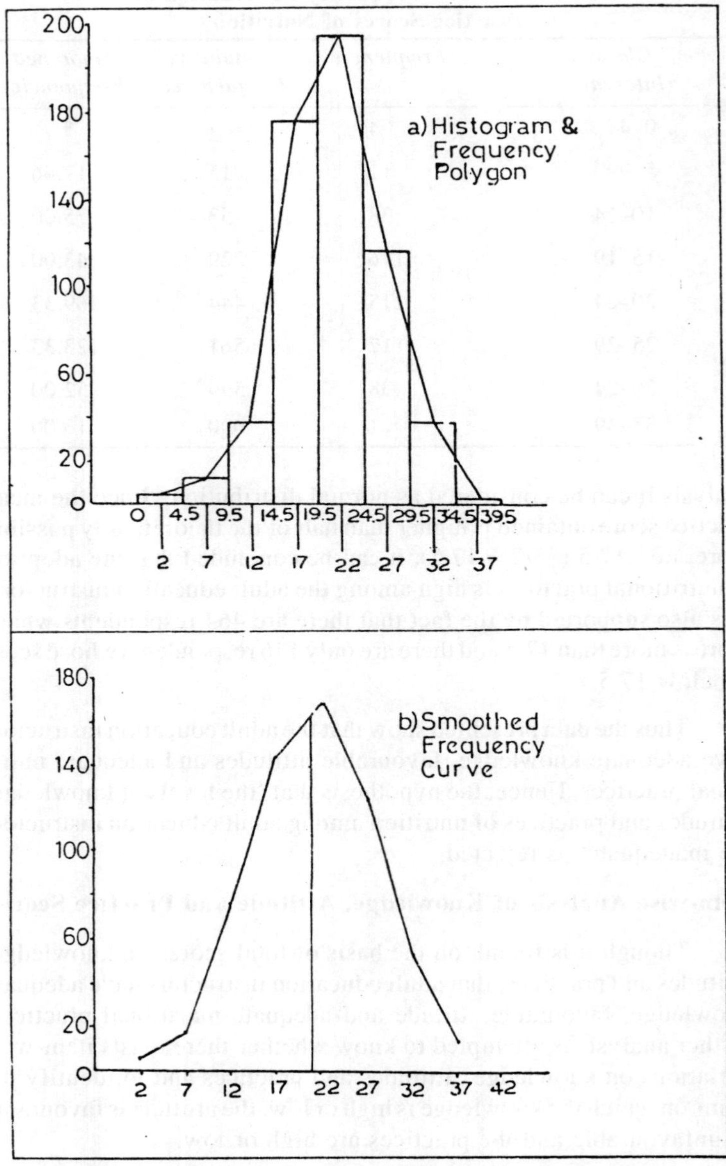

Fig. 5.3 : The Distribution of Practice Scores

Table 5.4 : Item-wise Knowledge of Instructors

S. No.	*Item No.*	*Description of the Item*	*Correct Responses*	*Wrong Responses*	*Proportions*
(1)	(2)	(3)	(4)	(5)	(6)
1.	18	Necessity of special diet for children if they are loosing their weight	559 (93.17)	41 (6.83)	0.931
2.	5.a	Need for taking extra amount of food by pregnant women	552 (92.00)	48 (8.00)	0 .920
3.	12	Need for supplementary food other than milk for infants after six months of age	538 (89.67)	62 (10.33)	0.896
4.	13.a	Different types of supplementary foods needed for infants	535 (89.17)	65 (10.83)	0.891
5.	15	Different types of foods needed in extra amounts for pre-school children	524 (87.33)	76 (12.67)	0.873
6.	11.a	Whether mother's milk is sufficient or not for infants whose age exceeds six months	523 (87.17)	77 (12.83)	0.871
7.	6	Different types of food needed in extra amounts for pregnant women	518 (86.33)	82 (13.67)	0.863
8.	17.c	Need for supplementary diet for children suffering from nutritional deficiency diseases	515 (85.83)	85 (14.17)	0.858
9.	4.b	Need for balanced diet for each individual everyday	512 (85.33)	88 (14.67)	0.853
10.	16	Whether it is good or not to give spicy foods for pre-school children	511 (85.17)	89 (14.83)	0.851
11.	22.a	Reasons for night blindness in children	497 (82.83)	103 (17.17)	0.828
12.	14.a	Type of special diet to be given to pre-school children	487 (81.17)	113 (18.83)	0.811
13.	33.b	Colour of egg yolk of an optimally cooked egg	483 (80.50)	117 (19.50)	0.805
14.	9.a	Different types of foods needed in extra amounts to lactating mothers	477 (79.50)	123 (20.50)	0.795

Contd...

Table 5.4 : Contd.

S. No.	*Item No.*	*Description of the Item*	*Correct Respon-ses*	*Wrong Respon-ses*	*Propor-tions*
(1)	(2)	(3)	(4)	(5)	(6)
15.	17.a	Whether diseases occur to children due to nutritionally deficient diet	472 (78.67)	128 (21.33)	0.786
16.	34	Need to preserve foodstuffs	458 (76.33)	142 (23.67)	0.763
17.	23	Different types of foods needed in extra amounts to children in order to protect them from night blindness	456 (76.00)	144 (24.00)	0.760
18.	7	Different types of foods required in extra amounts by pregnant women during last trimester	451 (75.17)	149 (24.83)	0.751
19.	9.b	Reason for taking extra amount of food by lactating mothers	448 (74.87)	152 (25.33)	0.746
20.	31.b	Reason for using baking soda while cooking dhals and vegetables	443 (73.83)	157 (26.17)	0.738
21.	31.a	Whether baking soda has to be used or not while cooking dhals and vegetables	438 (73.00)	162 (27.00)	0.730
22.	5.b	Reason for taking extra amount of food by pregnant women	425 (70.83)	175 (29.17)	0.708
23.	4.a	Meaning of balanced diet	424 (70.67)	176 (29.33)	0.706
24.	14.b	Reason for giving special diet for pre-school children	418 (69.67)	182 (30.33)	0.696
25.	10	Importance of mothers' first days milk 'cholestrum' for infants	409 (68.17)	191 (31.83)	0.681
26.	22.b	Symptoms of night blindness	407 (67.83)	193 (32.17)	0.678
27.	20.b	Chief symptoms of anaemia	404 (67.33)	196 (32.67)	0.673
28.	13.b	Reason for giving supplementary food for infants after six months of age	402 (67.00)	198 (33.00)	0.670

Contd...

Table 5.4 : Contd.

S. No.	*Item No.*	*Description of the Item*	*Correct Respon-ses*	*Wrong Respon-ses*	*Propor-tions*
(1)	(2)	(3)	(4)	(5)	(6)
29.	30.a	Whether vegetables and leafy vegetables have to be cooked in water for longer period	399 (66.50)	201 (33.50)	0.665
30.	1	Meaning of good food	398 (66.33)	202 (33.67)	0.663
31.	11.b	Reason for insufficiency of breast-milk for growing infants	396 (66.00)	204 (34.00)	0.660
32.	29	Method of cleaning vegetables and leafy vegetables	392 (65.33)	208 (34.67)	0.653
33.	17.b	Types of nutritional deficiency diseases	380 (63.33)	220 (36.67)	0.633
34.	30.b	Effect of Cooking vegetables and leafy vegetables in water for longer period	377 (62.83)	223 (37.17)	0.628
35.	33.a	Right method of cooking eggs	366 (61.00)	234 (39.00)	0.610
36.	32	Frequency of washing meat	365 (60.83)	235 (39.17)	0.608
37.	35.b	Reason for preservation of foodstuffs	363 (60.50)	237 (39.50)	0.605
38.	8	Frequency of taking excess amount of food by pregnant woman	341 (56.83)	259 (43.17)	0.568
39.	20.c	The category of people mostly affected by anaemia	321 (53.50)	279 (46.50)	0.535
40.	28.b	Reason for selecting pressure cooking as a best method for cooking rice	315 (52.50)	285 (47.50)	0.525
41.	27	Different types of foods rich in vitamin 'C'	304 (50.67)	296 (49.33)	0.506
42.	20.a	Reason for occurrence of anaemia	267 (44.50)	333 (55.50)	0.445
43.	26	Diseases caused due to vitamin 'C' deficiency	265 (44.17)	335 (55.83)	0.441

Contd...

Table 5.4 : Contd.

S. No.	*Item No.*	*Description of the Item*	*Correct Respon-ses*	*Wrong Respon-ses*	*Propor-tions*
(1)	(2)	(3)	(4)	(5)	(6)
44.	24	Diseases caused due to vitamin 'B' deficiency	245 (40.83)	355 (59.17)	0.408
45.	25	Different types of foods rich in Vitamin 'B'	244 (40.67)	356 (59.33)	0.406
46.	19	Different types of foods needed for children suffering from Kwashiorkor	243 (40.50)	357 (59.50)	0.405
47.	21	Different types of foods needed to prevent anaemia	221 (36.83)	379 (63.17)	0.368
48.	3	Chief function of foods like milk, pulses, oil seeds, meat, eggs, etc., for the body	208 (34.67)	392 (65.33)	0.346
49.	28.a	The best method of cooking rice	203 (33.83)	397 (66.17)	0.338
50.	2	Different types of foods required to be taken daily for good health	184 (30.67)	416 (69.33)	0.306
51.	35.a	Different methods of preserving foodstuffs	161 (26.83)	439 (73.17)	0.268

N.B. : Figures in paranthesis indicate the percentages.

Table 5.4 would reveal that the level of knowledge of instructors on each item is not same and there exists item-wise variations in knowledge.

An item which is checked by 50 per cent and more of the respondents is considered as an item on which the knowledge is high and other items are considered as the items on which the knowledge is less. Accordingly there are 41 items on which the knowledge is high and they are with Sl. Nos. 1 to 41. There are 10 items on which the knowledge is low and they are with Sl. Nos. 42 to 51.

While conducting training programmes to instructors the items on which there exists low knowledge should receive priority.

The frequencies, percentages and proportions of item-wise attitude towards nutrition of instructors, are shown in Table 5.5. A perusal of the Table would reveal that the level of attitude towards

Table 5.5 : Item-wise Attitude of Instructors

S. No.	*Item No.*	*Description of the Item*	*Agree* 3	*Uncert-ain* 2	*Dis-agree* 1	*Propor-tion*
(1)	(2)	(3)	(4)	(5)	(6)	(7)
1.	2	To be healthy, there is need to take foods like energy giving, body building and protective foods daily	538 (89.67)	24 (4.00)	38 (6.33)	2.883
2.	9.b	Lactating mothers have to extra amount of nutritious food to breast-fed and to safeguard her health	518 (86.33)	29 (4.83)	53 (8.83)	2.775
3.	13.b	For infants growth and nourishment, supplementary food should be given	515 (85.83)	34 (5.67)	51 (8.50)	2.773
4.	9.a	Nursing mothers need special foods such as milk, fruits, greens, fleshy foods, etc.	513 (85.50)	28 (4.67)	59 (9.83)	2.756
5.	5a	Pregnant women should consume more food	512 (85.33)	11 (1.83)	77 (12.83)	2.725
6.	12	After six months of age, infants should be given supplementary foods other than milk	501 (83.50)	21 (3.50)	78 (13.00)	2.705
7.	5.a	For blood sufficiency, health and foetal bone formation it is appropriate for pregnant women to take extra food	450 (75.00)	74 (12.33)	76 (12.67)	2.623
8.	14.b	Pre-school children's physical and mental development will depend on their good nutritious diet.	480 (80.00)	38 (6.33)	82 (13.67)	2.613
9.	17.a	Children will get diseases due to nutritionally deficient diet	446 (74.33)	57 (9.50)	97 (16.17)	2.581
10.	11.b	As the child grows the dietary requirements increase. Breast-milk alone will not cater to that needs	442 (73.67)	56 (9.33)	102 (17.00)	2.566

Contd...

Table 5.5 : Contd.

S. No.	*Item No.*	*Description of the Item*	*Agree* 3	*Uncert-ain* 2	*Dis-agree* 1	*Propor-tion*
(1)	(2)	(3)	(4)	(5)	(6)	(7)
11.	16	It is to give spicy foods for good health of pre-school children	437 (72.83)	56 (9.33)	107 (17.83)	2.550
12.	22.a	Night blindness in children is caused due to vitamin 'A' deficiency	430 (71.67)	68 (11.33)	102 (17.00)	2.546
13.	33.b	The colour of the egg yolk of an optimally cooked egg will be in yellow colour	435 (72.50)	32 (5.33)	133 (22.17)	2.503
14.	35.b	If the foodstuffs are preserved, they can be made use of in unseasonal periods	425 (70.83)	46 (7.67)	129 (21.50)	2.493
15.	27	Vitamin 'C' will be more in leafy vegetables, citrus fruits and in germinated fruits	413 (68.83)	66 (11.00)	121 (20.17)	2.486
16.	15	It is good to give milk, dhal, fleshy foods, eggs, greens, ragi, groundnut, etc., in extra amounts for pre-school children	416 (69.33)	55 (9.17)	129 (21.50)	2.478
17.	11.a	Mothers' milk is sufficient for growing infant whose age is less than six months	391 (65.71)	97 (16.17)	112 (18.67)	2.465
18.	19	There is need to give foods like ragi, greens, groundnut, dhal, etc., for children suffering from Kwashiorkor	401 (66.83)	75 (12.50)	124 (20.67)	2.461
19.	22.b	Reddishness and watering of eyes lead to night blindness	404 (67.33)	68 (11.33)	128 (21.33)	2.460
20.	20.c	Women and children are more affected by anaemia	405 (67.50)	63 (10.50)	132 (22.00)	2.455
21.	20.a	Anaemia is caused due to iron deficiency in the body	388 (64.67)	96 (16.00)	116 (19.33)	2.453

Contd...

Table 5.5 : (Contd.)

S. No.	*Item No.*	*Description of the Item*	*Agree* 3	*Uncert-ain* 2	*Dis-agree* 1	*Propor-tion*
(1)	(2)	(3)	(4)	(5)	(6)	(7)
22.	26	Sour tongue and bleeding of gums is due to vitamin 'C' deficiency	381 (65.00)	81 (13.50)	129 (21.50)	2.435
23.	24	Vitamin 'B' deficiency may be the reason for angular-stomatitis and glossitis	372 (62.00)	101 (16.83)	127 (21.17)	2.408
24.	31.b	Usage of baking soda in cooking the vegetables and dhal increases the nutritive value	376 (62.67)	88 (14.67)	136 (22.67)	2.400
25.	18	There is no need to give special diet if children are becoming weak and loosing their weight	381 (63.50)	51 (8.50)	168 (28.00)	2.355
26.	32	Meat can be washed any number of times	367 (61.17)	53 (8.83)	180 (30.00)	2.313
27.	23	There is no need to give special foodstuffs for child-ren in order to protect them from night blindness	358 (59.67)	68 (11.33)	174 (29.00)	2.306
28.	33.a	It is not good to boil eggs for longer duration	369 (61.50)	43 (7.17)	188 (31.33)	2.301
29.	1	Preparations with lot of oil and ghee are good food	326 (54.33)	112 (18.67)	162 (27.00)	2.273
30.	31.a	It is not good to use baking soda while cooking vegetables and dhal	350 (58.33)	50 (8.33)	200 (33.33)	2.250
31.	30.a	Leafy vegetables and vege-tables should not be cooked in water for longer period	344 (57.33)	55 (9.17)	201 (33.50)	2.238
32.	14.a	There is no need to give spe-cial diet for pre-school children	349 (58.17)	41 (6.83)	210 (35.00)	2.231

Contd...

Table 5.5 : (Contd.)

S. No.	*Item No.*	*Description of the Item*	*Agree* 3	*Uncert-ain* 2	*Dis-agree* 1	*Propor-tion*
(1)	(2)	(3)	(4)	(5)	(6)	(7)
33.	13.a	Fruits, fruit juices, dhal, fish liver oils, milk poridge, egg yolk, boiled vegetables, greens, etc., should not be given for infants	340 (56.67)	57 (9.50)	203 (33.83)	2.228
34.	17.c	There is no need to give supplementary diet for children suffering from nutritional deficiency diseases	324 (54.00)	78 (13.00)	198 (33.00)	2.210
35.	6	Pregnant women need not consume special foods such as milk, fruits, greens, varieties of cereals, dhals, etc.	320 (53.33)	75 (12.50)	205 (34.17)	2.191
36.	35.a	Foodstuffs will not get spoiled if they are preserved in air tight place	330 (55.00)	50 (8.33)	220 (36.67)	2.183
37.	21	There is no need to give foods like ragi, jaggery, leafy vegetables, dried fruits, etc., for people suffering from anaemia	309 (51.50)	91 (15.16)	200 (33.34)	2.181
38.	17.b	Kwashiorkor and anaemia diseases caused to children are not due to nutritional deficiency	295 (49.17)	112 (18.67)	193 (32.17)	2.170
39.	34	There is no need to preserve the foodstuffs	314 (52.33)	40 (6.67)	246 (41.00)	2.113
40.	25	Consumption of hand pounded rice, ragi, bajra cannot prevent vitamin 'B' deficiency	256 (47.67)	90 (15.00)	224 (37.33)	2.103
41.	20.b	Paleness, loss of appetite, breathlessness, ditches in nailes, tiresomeness are not the symptoms of anaemia	287 (47.83)	85 (14.17)	228 (38.00)	2.098

Contd...

Table 5.5 : (Contd.)

S. No.	*Item No.*	*Description of the Item*	*Agree* 3	*Uncert-ain* 2	*Dis-agree* 1	*Propor-tion*
(1)	(2)	(3)	(4)	(5)	(6)	(7)
42.	10	Mother's first days milk 'cholestrum' is not good for infants	299 (49.83)	58 (9.67)	243 (40.50)	2.093
43.	4.b	Every person need not take balanced diet every day	246 (41.00)	106 (17.67)	248 (41.33)	1.996
44.	28.b	There is no change in the nutritive value if the rice is cooked by any method	260 (43.33)	73 (12.17)	267 (44.50)	1.988
45.	8	Pregnant woman should take her diet many times and in excess quantities	256 (42.67)	74 (12.33)	270 (45.00)	1.976
46.	28.a	Rice draining is the best method	261 (43.50)	54 (9.00)	285 (47.50)	1.960
47.	7	It is not good, to consume extra amounts of greens, fruits, dhal, etc., by pregnant women during last trimester	258 (43.00)	57 (9.50)	285 (47.50)	1.955
48.	4.a	Costly diet is not a balanced diet	220 (36.67)	132 (22.00)	248 (41.33)	1.953
49.	3	Everyday there is no need to take foods like meat, milk, dhal, oil seeds, eggs, etc., for body building and growth	234 (39.00)	67 (11.17)	299 (49.83)	1.891
50.	30.b	If the vegetables and leafy vegetables are cooked in water for longer period, it will get digested easily	194 (32.33)	57 (9.50)	349 (58.17)	1.741
51.	29	While cooking, it is better to wash the vegetables and leafy vegetables after cutting	182 (30.33)	33 (5.50)	385 (64.17)	1.661

N.B. : Figures in paranthesis indicate the percentages.

each item of nutrition is not same and there exists item-wise variations in attitudes.

The scores on an attitude item varies from 1 to 3—1 for disagree, 2 for uncertain and 3 for agree. The items which received 2.00 and above average score (proportion) are considered as the items on which there is high favourable attitude and the rest of the items are treated as those unfavourable attitude. According to this criteria, there are 42 items on which the attitude is favourable and they are with Sl. Nos. 1 to 42. The nine items on which the attitude is unfavourable are with Sl. Nos. 43 to 51.

Table 5.5(a) gives the item-wise nutritional practices of instructors in terms of frequencies, percentages and proportions. It is evident from the Table that the level of practice of instructors on each item is not same and there exists item-wise variations in practices.

An item which is checked by 50 per cent and more of the respondents is considered as an item on which the practice is high and other items are considered as the items on which the practice is poor. Accordingly there are 24 items on which the practice is high and they are with Sl. Nos. 1 to 24. There are 11 items on which the practice is poor and they are with Sl. Nos. 25 to 35.

Table 5.5a : Item-wise Practices of Instructors

S. No.	*Item No.*	*Description of the Item*	*Correct Responses*	*Wrong Responses*	*Proportions*
(1).	(2)	(3)	(4)	(5)	(6)
1.	14	Nutritious food is given to pre-school children	562 (93.67)	38 (6.33)	0.936
2.	12	Supplementary food other than milk for children after six months of age is provided	532 (88.67)	68 (11.33)	0.886
3.	13	Different types of supplementary foods for infants after six months of age are given	524 (87.33)	76 (12.67)	0.873
4.	18	Special diet is offered for children if they are loosing their weight	521 (86.83)	79 (13.17)	0.868
5.	15	Different types of foodstuffs in extra amounts for pre-school children are supplied	516 (86.00)	84 (14.00)	0.860

Contd...

Table 5.5a : contd.

S. No.	*Item No.*	*Description of the Item*	*Correct Respon-ses*	*Wrong Respon-ses*	*Propor-tions*
(1)	(2)	(3)	(4)	(5)	(6)
6.	5	Extra amount of food is taken by pregnant women	508 (84.67)	92 (15.33)	0.846
7.	16	Pre-school children are not provided with spicy foods	487 (81.17)	113 (18.83)	0.811
8.	11	Supplementary food is not given to infants less than six months of age	477 (79.50)	123 (20.50)	0.795
9.	31	Baking soda is not used in cooking dhals and vegetables	467 (77.83)	133 (22.17)	0.778
10.	9	Lactating mothers are taking differ-types of foods in extra amounts	466 (77.67)	134 (22.33)	0.776
11.	6	Different types of foods in extra amounts are consumed by pregnant women	462 (77.00)	138 (23.00)	0.770
12.	17	Supplementary food is provided for children when they have nutritional deficiency diseases	456 (76.00)	144 (24.00)	0.760
13.	34	Foodstuffs are preserved	403 (67.17)	197 (32.83)	0.671
14.	10	Mothers' first days milk 'cholestrum' is given to infants	400 (66.67)	200 (33.33)	0.666
15.	1	Nutritive value is given preference while selecting good food	383 (63.83)	217 (36.17)	0.638
16.	4	Balanced diet is taken everyday (63.00)	378 (37.00)	222	0.630
17.	29	Vegetables and leafy vegetables are washed before cutting and cooking	377 (62.83)	233 (37.17)	0.628
18.	3	Everyday any one of the foodstuffs like milk, dhal, oil seeds, meat, eggs, etc. is taken	365 (60.83)	235 (39.17)	0.608
19.	8	Pregnant women are taking food many times in small quantities	356 (59.33)	244 (40.67)	0.593

Contd...

Table 5.5a : contd.

S. No.	*Item No.*	*Description of the Item*	*Correct Respon-ses*	*Wrong Respon-ses*	*Propor-tions*
(1)	(2)	(3)	(4)	(5)	(6)
20.	2	Any one foodstuff from each of the following three food groups is taken everyday 1) Rice, Ragi, Bajra, Sugar, Jaggery 2) Milk, dhal, oil seeds, fleshy foods, eggs, etc. 3) Leafy vegetables, vegetables, fruits	352 (58.67)	248 (41.33)	0.586
21.	32	Meat is wahsed once in clean water to remove dirt	328 (54.67)	272 (45.33)	0.546
22.	30	Vegetables and leafy vegetables are not cooked for longer period	325 (54.17)	275 (45.83)	0.541
23.	33	Eggs are cooked in boiling water for 8 or 10 minutes and cooled imme-diately	312 (52.00)	288 (48.00)	0.520
24.	20	Symptoms are observed in people suffering from anaemia and identified	302 (50.33)	298 (49.67)	0.503
25.	22	Observed and identified people suff-ering from night blindness	298 (49.67)	302 (50.33)	0.496
26.	23	To prevent night blindness foodstuffs given include greens, fruits like papayya and mango, yellow vegeta-bles like carrot, etc., milk, fish	282 (47.00)	318 (53.00)	0.470
27.	24	People suffering from angularsto-matitis and glossitits are watched and spotted	264	336	0.440
28.	7	High quantities of greens, dhal, fruits are given to pregnant women during last trimester	262 (43.67)	338 (56.33)	0.436
29.	19	Ragi, greens, groundnuts, dhal are given to the children to prevent them from Kwashiorkor	256 (42.67)	344 (57.33)	0.426
30.	26	People suffering from sour tongue and bleeding of gums are noticed and recognised	236 (39.33)	364 (60.67)	0.393

Contd...

Table 5.5a : contd.

S. No.	*Item No.*	*Description of the Item*	*Correct Respon- ses*	*Wrong Respon- ses*	*Propor- tions*
(1)	(2)	(3)	(4)	(5)	(6)
31.	21	Ragi, Greens, Jaggery, dried fruits are given to people to prevent them from anaemia	192 (32.00)	408 (68.00)	0.320
32.	27	Leafy vegetables, citrus fruits, germinated pulses are given to people for prevention of sour tongue and bleeding of gums	172 (28.67)	428 (71.33)	0.286
33.	25	To prevent angularstomatitis and glossitis, hand pounded rice, ragi bajra are given	152 (25.33)	448 (74.67)	0.253
34.	28	Pressure cooking method is followed for cooking rice	144 (24.00)	456 (76.00)	0.240
35.	35	Foodstuffs are preserved in the form of pickling, sundrying, salting, sugar syruping	124 (20.67)	476 (79.33)	0.206

N.B. : Figures in paranthesis indicate the percentages.

While conducting training programmes to instructors, the items on which there exists unfavourable attitude and low practice should receive priority.

Thus, the results indicate that the hypothesis 'there exists variations in the level of knowledge, attitudes and practices on different items of nutrition among adult education instructors', is tenablé.

Section 2

Influence of Independent Variables on Dependent Variables

The influence of various socio, economic and demographic variables on the dependent variables, namely, knowledge, attitudes and practices of nutrition among adult education instructors is studied by considering each of the independent variables separately. The influence of independent variables on the three dependent variables, viz., knowledge, attitudes and practices of nutrition is discussed under three parts separately.

Knowledge of Nutrition

In this part, the influence of the sixteen socio, economic and demographic factors on knowledge of nutrition is examined by employing 't' test, ANOVA and Kramer's multiple range test. The sixteen socio, economic and demographic variables include (1) Age, (2) Sex, (3) Annual Income, (4) Caste, (5) Religion, (6) Marital Status, (7) Occupation, (8) Education Status, (9) Family Type, (10) Size of the Family, (11) Experience, (12) Newspaper, (13) Radio, (14) Films, (15) Filmshows and (16) Television. Each of them is considered separately to highlight its effect on the level of knowledge of nutrition.

Age and Knowledge of Nutrition

Age is considered as a social factor (Roy and Kapur, 1975; Roy, 1971). It is also considered as a bio-social factor. It is frequently classified under demographic factors. In a rural setting chronological age is considered in many social situations. Other things being equal, people of older age group are preferred to head families, to settle marriages, to negotiate and even to provide leadership. Age is also related to intelligence, maturity, perception and aspiration. Some past investigations have shown that ability to learn increases from early childhood to about twenty five years of age and decreases gradually thereafter. Thorndike et al., (1928) studied the learning process and the changes in the ability of persons to learn upto the age group of 45 years. In their experiments childhood was found to be emphatically not the best age for learning, when measured in terms of returns per unit of time span.

According to Roy and Kapur (1975) the best age for learning is the twenties and any age below 45 is better than age-group 10–14. There is no conclusive evidence to generalize that age has positive relationship with knowledge. Further, there is no single study indicating the relationship of age and knowledge of nutrition among adult education instructors. Of the total respondents of 600, 23.17 (139) per cent of them are below 20 years of age, 26.83 (161) per cent are in 21–25 age group, 19.17 (115) per cent are in 26–30 age group and 30.83 (185) per cent belong to above 30 years age group. Their knowledge scores were analysed to find out the differences among them. The mean scores, standard deviation and number of subjects in each of the four groups are presented in the following Table.

Table 5.6 : Means (M) and Standard Deviations (SD) of Knowledge Scores of Instructors of Different Age Groups

Age group in years	*N*	*M*	*SD*
Less than 20	139	32.7122	6.2227
21 – 25	161	33.1801	7.1591
26 – 30	115	34.0261	7.3348
Above 30	185	34.8811	7.0509

An observation of the means indicates that the instructors in the age group of above 30 years are superior and those in the age group of less than 20 years are inferior to others in knowledge scores. The summary of analysis of variance shown in Table 5.7 discloses whether these differences are significant.

Table 5.7 : Summary of ANOVA of Knowledge Scores of Instructors of Different Age-groups

Source of Variance	*df*	*Sum of squares*	*Mean of squares*	'F'
Between groups	3	447.375	149.125	3.0628*
Within groups	596	29018.56	48.6888	
Total	**599**	**29465.935**		

Note : * indicates significant at 0.05 level; ** indicates significant at 0.01 level; NS indicates not significant. The same notations are used in the following tables.

As the 'F' ratio is significant at 0.05 level of probability for 3, 596 degrees of freedom, the null hypothesis that 'there would be no significant influence of age on knowledge of nutrition among adult education instructors' is rejected. It is concluded that the age of the instructor is a significant factor in influencing the knowledge of nutrition. An observation of the mean scores indicates that instructors in the age group of above 30 years appear to have more knowledge. Probably, the lower age group instructors have low knowledge on nutrition because of their less experience. It is quite natural that the older respondents might have had more opportunities to acquire knowledge of nutrition during their life time than young people.

To find out which of the mean scores of the four groups differ significantly from the others in the level of their knowledge, 't' test or some other test may be employed. In the present investigation, Kramer's extension of multiple range test to group means with unequal numbers (Kramer, 1956) which is considered to be a more appropriate test, was employed and the results are shown in Table 5.8.

Table 5.8 : Results of Kramer's Test Applied to Find the Significance of the Difference Among the Means of the Knowledge Scores of Instructors Classified According to their Age

	Less than 20 years	*21 – 25 years*	*26 – 30 years*	*More than 30 years*
N	139	161	115	185
M	32.7122	33.1801	34.0261	34.8811

Note : 1. Any two means *not underscored* by the same line *are* significantly different.

2. Any two means *underscored* by the same line *are not* significantly different.

3. The means are arranged in ascending order from left to right. The level of significance employed in applying the Kramer's test is 0.05 level.

The results of the Kramer's test presented in the above Table reveal that there is a significant difference in the knowledge between those who are less than 20 years and those who are more than 30 years and also between those who are in 21–25 years and those who are more than 30 years. That means the instructors whose age is less than 25 years are possessing less knowledge of nutrition compared to those whose age is more than 30 years.

Sex and Knowledge of Nutrition

Sex has proved to be a variable in many types of learning

situations. As far as the relationship between sex and knowledge of nutrition of the adult education instructors is concerned, it is not adequately enquired. Hence, sex is included to see whether there would be any difference in the knowledge of nutrition between males and females. Suppose, the instructors of one sex group prove to be better in their knowledge than the other, then remedial action may be taken to see that the handicapped group makes up its deficiency. There are 329 males and 271 females in the present study and sex-wise differences in knowledge are presented below.

Table 5.9 : Sex-wise Differences in Knowledge of Nutrition

Sex	*N*	*M*	*SD*	*'t' value*
Male	329	32.769	6.2521	3.7832**
Female	271	34.959	7.6579	

** indicates significant at 0.01 level

A perusal of the Table 5.9 makes it clear that the difference between the means pertaining to the knowledge in nutrition of males and females is significant (The 't' value is significant at 0.01 level of probability for 598 df). Among the two means, the mean of females (34.959) is more than that of the mean of the males (32.769). Hence, evidently it may be said that females possess more knowledge of nutrition as compared to males. A probable reason for this may be that females are more concerned with food and nourishment at every stage than males. Hence, females might have acquired more knowledge of nutrition.

Therefore, the null hypothesis that 'there would be significant difference between the knowledge of males and females about nutrition' is rejected.

Annual Income and Knowledge of Nutrition

The relationship of income with many social, economic and demographic factors has been established by many studies. Higher income of an individual enables him to have various things like Radio, T.V., Newspaper and as a result he/she might have acquired more knowledge of nutrition. In order to understand the relationship between family annual income and the knowledge of nutrition the respondents are divided into four broad categories on the basis of the annual income of the family. Accordingly, 115 respondents fall in the less than Rs. 2,500 income group, 166 in the Rs. 2,501 to 3,500 group, 189 in the Rs. 3,501 to 4,500 group and the remaining 130 fall in the income group of above Rs. 4,500 per annum. The relationship between income and knowledge is shown in Table 5.10.

It is evident from Table 5.10 that the instructors belonging to 3,501–4,500 group are having more knowledge about nutrition than the other three groups. Analysis of variance was employed to test whether there was any significant difference among the mean scores of the four groups.

Table 5.10 : Mean and SDs of Knowledge Scores of Different Sub-groups of Instructors Classified According to their Income (Rupees per annum)

Income group	*N*	*M*	*SD*
Less than 2,500	115	33.8956	7.0048
2,501 – 3,500	166	32.3554	6.3055
3,501 – 4,500	189	34.7460	6.9144
Above 4,500	130	33.9923	7.6796

Table 5.11 : Summary of ANOVA of Knowledge Scores of Instructors from Families of Varied Income Groups

Source of Variance	*df*	*Sum of squares*	*Mean of squares*	*'F'*
Between groups	3	520.3125	173.4375	
				3.5711*
Within groups	596	28945.63	48.5665	
Total	**599**	**29465.9425**		

* indicates significant at 0.05 level

The results indicate that the annual income of the family of the instructor is a significant factor which influence the knowledge of nutrition (F = 3.5711, P 0.05). Hence, the null hypothesis, is rejected.

To find out which income group of instructors differed significantly from the others in the extent of their knowledge scores, Kramer's (1956) test was employed.

It may be seen from the Table 5.12 that the instructors whose income was Rs. 2,501–3,500 obtained a mean score of 32.3554 and they are the low knowledgeable and differed significantly from the instructors whose income was Rs. 3,501–4,500.

Table 5.12 : Results of Kramer's Test Applied to Find the Significance of the Difference Among the Mean Knowledge Scores of Instructors Classified According to their Family Income

	2,501--3,500 M_2	*Less than 2,500* M_1	*Above 4,500* M_4	*3,501–4,500* M_5
N	166	115	130	189
M	32.3554	33.8956	33.9923	34.7460
	————	————	————	————
		————	————	
	————	————	————	
		————	————	————

Note : 1. Any two means *not underscored* by the same line *are* significantly different.

2. Any two means *underscored* by the same line are *not* significantly different.

3. The means are arranged in ascending order from left to right

4. The level of significance employed in applying th Kramer's test is 0.05 level.

Caste and Knowledge of Nutrition

Caste is not an Indian word. In its original form, 'casta', belongs to the Portugese, by whom it was ordinarily used among themselves to express 'cast', 'mould', 'race', 'kind' and 'quality'. It was applied by the Portugese, when they first arrived in the East, to designate the peculiar system of religious and social distinctions which they observed among the Hindu people.

Caste gives sanction for recognition, acceptance, conservation and sacramental dedication and vice-versa of a human being on his appearance in the world. The individual behaviour with respect to eating, reading and listening are affected by caste (Wilson, 1976). Historically the Indian society is stratified into a hierarchy of castes. It curtails social mobility and perpetuates socio-economic inequality. Caste still retains its pivotal position in the social structure of the Indian village. Of the total respondents 161 belongs to Forward Caste, 248 belongs to Backward Caste and 191 belongs to Scheduled Castes and Scheduled Tribes. Table 5.13 presents knowledge scores of nutrition among various caste groups.

By observing the trend in the mean scores, it appears that the forward caste group instructors are having more knowledge than the others. To see whether they differ significantly, analysis of variance technique was applied. The summary of analysis of variance is given in Table 5.14.

Table 5.13 : Mean and SDs of Knowledge Scores of Instructors of Different Caste Groups

Caste group	*N*	*M*	*SD*
Forward Caste	161	35.0186	6.7589
Backward Caste	248	33.7298	7.1123
Scheduled Castes/ Scheduled Tribes	191	32.7329	6.9060

Table 5.14 : Summary of ANOVA of Knowledge Scores of Instructors of Different Caste-groups

Source of Variance	*df*	*Sum of squares*	*Mean of squares*	*'F'*
Between groups	2	456.6875	228.3438	4.6992**
Within groups	597	29009.25	48.5917	
Total	**599**	**29465.9375**		

** indicates significant at 0.01 level

The results in the above Table indicate that there is significant difference between the mean scores of different caste groups at 0.01 level. Therefore, the null hypothesis, is rejected. It is concluded that the caste of the instructor has influence on the nutrition knowledge. Also it is evident that the mean score of Scheduled Caste/Scheduled Tribes is lower than those of the other groups. The probable reason for this is the oppressed status of the community in the society resulting into less opportunity to develop their knowledge.

However, to know between which groups the difference is significant, Kramer's multiple range test is employed and the results are presented in the Table 5.15.

It is clear from the Table 5.15 that the Scheduled Caste/

Scheduled Tribes differed significantly from Forward Caste.

Table 5.15 : Results of Kramer's Test Applied to Find the Significance of the Difference Among the Mean Knowledge Scores of Instructors of Different Caste Group

	Scheduled Caste/ Scheduled Tribe M_3	*Backward Caste* M_2	*Forward Caste* M_1
N	191	248	161
M	32.7329	33.7298	35.0186

Note : 1. Any two means *not underscored* by the same line *are* significantly different.

2. Any two means *underscored* by the same line are *not* significantly different.

3. The means are arranged in ascending order from left to right

4. The level of significance employed in applying the Kramer's test is 0.05 level.

Religion and Knowledge of Nutrition

Religion is the most influential force of social control, but also the most effective guide to human behaviour. In a traditional society and particularly in India, religion has a pervasive influence which extend practically to all aspects of life. In the present study 87.88 per cent of the respondents are Hindus, 6.67 per cent Muslims and 5.5 per cent are Christians. Table 5.16 presents the means and other statistics of various religious groups.

Table 5.16 : Mean and SDs of Knowledge Scores of Instructors of Varied Religions

Religion	*N*	*M*	*SD*
Hindus	527	33.8994	7.1032
Muslims	40	33.10000	5.5263
Christians	33	32.3030	6.8688

The mean scores show a negligible variation among the three groups with regard to their knowledge in nutrition. The ANOVA technique was employed to see whether there exists any significant differences among the three means and the results are shown in Table 5.17.

Table 5.17 : Summary of ANOVA of Knowledge Scores of Instructors of Different Religions

Source of Variance	*df*	*Sum of squares*	*Mean of squares*	*'F'*
Between groups	2	97.6875	48.8438	0.9929^{NS}
Within groups	597	·29368.25		
Total	**599**	**29465.9375**		

NS–indicates not significant

As the 'F' ratio calculated is far below the Table value even at 0.05 level of significance for 2 and 597 df, the null hypothesis that 'there would not be significant influence of religion on knowledge of nutrition', is retained. In other words, it is concluded that the religion has no influence on the level of knowledge of nutrition.

Marital Status and Knowledge of Nutrition

Unlike sex or age, marital status is not a biological but socially acquired characteristic. The study of population by marital status in relation to their knowledge of nutrition is useful for several reasons. Marital status of a person may be a promoter or demoter of the acquisition of knowledge of nutrition. Married people may be possessing more knowledge of nutrition than unmarried people in some settings, while the contrary may be true in other settings. There are 317 married and 283 unmarried instructors in the sample. To test whether there is significant difference between the married and unmarried instructors in their knowledge of nutrition, 't' test was employed. The mean scores, standard deviations of the both the groups with the results of 't' test are shown in the Table 5.18.

The calculated 't' value is significant beyond 0.01 level. Hence the null hypothesis, is rejected. If we observe the mean scores of the two groups, it is evident that the married instructors obtained higher mean (34.5016) score than unmarried (32.9258). It may be due to the fact that the married people are more involved in sharing the family

Table 5.18 : Mean and SDs of Knowledge Scores of Married and Unmarried Instructors and the 't' Value for Difference Between Two Means

Marital Status	*N*	*Mean*	*SD*	*'t' value*
Married	317	34.5016	7.1758	2.7773**
Unmarried	283	32.9258	6.7178	

** indicates significant at 0.01 level

functions along with their counterparts (women are more knowledgeable than men, vide Table 5.9), than unmarried respondents and also due to the higher average age of married instructors the marital status has positive influence on knowledge. (Higher the age, higher was the knowledge in nutrition, vide Table 5.6). The results indicate that marital status of the subjects has a significant bearing on their level of knowledge in nutrition.

Occupation and Knowledge of Nutrition

Theoretically occupation is directly related to the acquisition of knowledge and understanding. This is for the reason that occupational groups would be more interested in acquiring knowledge and understanding in their respective occupations. To know the type of relationship, occupation is included in the present study. Table 5.19 shows the relationship between occupation and knowledge of nutrition. Occupationally, the adult education instructors are engaged in diversified occupations. They are classified into four broad occupational groups, viz., agriculture, caste occupants, self-employed/business and others (students, unemployed educated youth, unmarried girls, etc.). Occupation-wise differences in knowledge are shown in Table 5.19.

From the Table it can be seen that the instructors with agriculture occupation have lower knowledge compared to instructors of other

Table 5.19 : Occupation-wise Differences in Knowledge of Nutrition

Occupation Group	*N*	*M*	*SD*
Agriculture	206	32.5437	6.5386
Caste Occupants	114	33.4123	6.6423
Self-employment/Business	123	35.6342	7.3188
Others	157	34.1338	7.2570

occupation groups. The differences between the means indicate that there exists significant differences within the groups. The summary of analysis of variance presented in Table 5.20 reveals the same.

Table 5.20 : Summary of ANOVA of Knowledge Scores of Instructors of Different Occupations

Source of Variance	*df*	*Sum of squares*	*Mean of squares*	*'F'*
Between groups	3	772.4375	257.4972	5.3482**
Within groups	596	28693.50	48.1435	
Total	**599**	**29465.9375**		

** indicates significant at 0.01 level

As 'F' ratio is significant at 0.01 level, the null hypothesis, is rejected. It is proved that occupation of the instructor is a significant factor influencing the level of knowledge on nutrition. A perusal of the mean scores indicate that instructors engaged in self-employed/business appeared to possess more knowledge because of their wider exposure to various issues and cordial contacts with numerous persons.

Table 5.21 : Results of Kramer's Test Applied to Find the Significance of the Difference Among the Mean Knowledge Scores of Instructors Classified According to their Occupations

	Agriculture M_1	*Caste Occupants* M_2	*Others* M_4	*Self-employment/ Business* M_3
N	206	114	157	123
M	32.5437	33.4123	34.1338	35.6342

Note : 1. Any two means *not underscored* by the same line *are* significantly different.

2. Any two means *underscored* by the same line are *not significantly* different.

3. The means are arranged in ascending order from left to right.

4. The level of significance employed in applying the Kramer's test is 0.05 level.

To find out which occupation groups differ significantly from the others in the extent of their knowledge scores Kramer's multiple range test was employed.

It is evident from the Table 5.21 that the agriculturists are possessing significantly less knowledge than the last two groups, viz., self-employment/business and others and also the caste occupants are possessing significantly low knowledge on nutrition than self-employed/business people.

Educational Status and Knowledge of Nutrition

According to the educational qualifications of the subjects, the total sample is divided into four groups—instructors with 8 years of schooling, with 10 years of schooling, 12 years of schooling and above 12 years of schooling. Table 5.22 provides the mean knowledge scores, standard deviations and the number of subjects in each category of educational status.

Table 5.22 : Means and SDs of Knowledge Scores of Instructors with Varied Educational Backgrounds

Qualification Category	*N*	*M*	*SD*
8 years of schooling	63	31.6825	7.6570
10 years of schooling	348	32.7586	7.0429
12 years of schooling	143	35.8951	6.3639
Above 12 years of schooling	46	37.5217	4.1585

The trend of mean scores indicate that the educational qualification is positively related to knowledge scores, i.e., higher the educational qualification, higher is the mean score of knowledge. The results of analysis of variance given in Table 5.23 also indicate that the influence of education on the level of knowledge is highly significant.

As the calculated 'F' value is higher than the Table value for 3, 596 df, at 0.01 level, the null hypothesis is rejected. Hence, it can be concluded that the instructors with higher qualification possess more knowledge.

However, to know among which two groups the difference is significant, Kramer's multiple range test is employed and the results are presented in the Table 5.24.

Table 5.23 : Summary of ANOVA of Knowledge of Instructors with varied Educational Qualifications

Source of Variance	*df*	*Sum of squares*	*Mean of squares*	*'F'*
Between the groups	3	1923.625	641.2083	13.8754**
Within groups	596	27542.31	46.2119	
Total	**599**	**29465.935**		

** indicates significant at 0.01 level

Table 5.24 : Results of Kramer's Test Applied to Find the Significance of the Difference Among the Mean Knowledge Scores of Instructors of Different Educational Qualifications

	8 years of schooling Group I M_1	*10 years of schooling Group II M_2*	*12 years of schooling Group III M_3*	*Above 12 years of schooling Group IV M_4*
N	63	348	143	46
M	31.6825	32.7586	35.8951	37.5217

Note : 1. Any two means *not underscored* by the same line *are* significantly different.

2. Any two means *underscored* by the same line are *not* significantly different.

3. The means are arranged in ascending order from left to right.

4. The level of significance employed in applying the Kramer's test is 0.05 level.

From the above Table, it can be seen that the differences in the knowledge of nutrition between 1st and 2nd groups and 3rd and 4th groups are not statistically significant and the other mean differences, viz., M_1 and M_3, M_1 and M_4, M_2 and M_3 and M_2 and M_4 are statistically significant. There is a difference between two groups possessing 8 or 10 years of schooling and 12 or above 12 years of schooling.

Therefore, the adult education authorities should prefer more qualified people as instructors to carry on the task of adult education and to achieve the fundamental objectives of the adult education programme, viz., literacy, functionality and awareness. At present the minimum qualification required for an adult education instructor is 8 years of schooling. In the light of the above results the minimum qualifications should be enhanced to atleast more than 10 years of schooling.

Family Type and Knowledge of Nutrition

Joint family is also one of the basic social institutions in India particularly in rural India. In urban areas, a joint family is giving place to the nuclear family. The type of family is an important determinant in many aspects that pertain to human behaviour. For various reasons a respondent living in a joint family may have more leisure or no leisure at all and as such, he/she may/may not have time to acquire knowledge of nutrition. Hence the type of the family as a variable is included in the present study. Of the total respondents, 413 belong to joint family and 187 to nuclear family. The results found in Table 5.25 show that the respondents living in nuclear family possess more knowledge of nutrition than the respondents living in joint family.

Table 5.25 : Means and SDs of Knowledge Scores of Different Type of Families

Family Type	*N*	*M*	*SD*	*'t' value*
Joint	413	33.2373	6.7646	
				2.6344**
Nuclear	187	34.9091	7.3882	

** indicates significant at 0.01 level

It is plausible that the nuclear family system provides scope for learning various matters of nutrition because of close association between wife and husband and proper planning in all aspects of family development and successful implementation of their plans for the welfare of the family.

Hence, the null hypothesis, namely, that 'there would not be significant influence of the type of the family of the instructors on their knowledge of nutrition', is rejected.

Size of the Family and Knowledge of Nutrition

Family size of a respondent is the number of children he/she possess. Family size may be either positively or negatively correlated with the acquisition and possession of knowledge of nutrition. An instructor from a large family may acquire and possess more knowledge of nutrition, for he might afford much leisure, interaction with the people and exposure to training programme. On the other hand, an instructor might lag behind in the knowledge, for in a large family every member might have tight work and/or many responsibilities that leave no time for him to concentrate on his acquisition of knowledge of nutrition. Of the total sample of respondents, 139 have less than 4 family size, 193 have 5–6 size, 125 have 7–8 size and remaining 108 have above 8 members of the family size. Their knowledge scores were analysed to find out the differences among them. The mean scores, standard deviations and number of subjects in each of the four groups are presented in theTable 5.26.

Table 5.26 : Means and Standard Deviations of Knowledge Scores of Instructors of Different Family Size Groups

Family Size	*N*	*M*	*SD*
Less than 4	174	34.9885	6.8380
5 – 6	193	34.1917	6.8151
7 – 8	125	32.5520	7.0987
Above 8	108	32.3982	7.0618

The means scores of the above table reveal that instructors with less than four members of family size are possessing more knowledge and next follows the instructors with family of 5–6 members. The instructors with families above 8 members are having very low knowledge of nutrition. The summary of analysis of variance shown below discloses whether these differences are significant.

The results in the Table 5.27 indicate that there is significant difference between the mean knowledge scores of the four groups (F = 4.7023 for 3 and 596 df). Therefore, the null hypothesis is rejected. It is concluded that the family size is associated with the knowledge of nutrition. However, the analysis is further carried on to test the significant difference between the different sets of two groups. Kramer's multiple range test is employed and the results are presented in Table 5.28.

Table 5.27 : Summary of ANOVA of Knowledge Scores of Different Family Groups of Instructors

Source of Variance	*df*	*Sum of squares*	*Mean of squares*	*'F'*
Between groups	3	681.3125	227.1042	4.7023**
Within groups	596	28784.63	48.2964	
Total	**599**	**29465.9425**		

** indicates significant at 0.01 level

Table 5.28 : Results of Kramer's Test Applied to Find the Significance of the Difference Among the Mean Knowledge Scores of Instructors of Different Family Sizes

	Above 8 Members M_4	*7–8* M_3	*5–6* M_2	*Less than 4* M_1
N	108	123	193	174
M	32.3982	32.5520	34.1917	34.9885

Note : 1. Any two means *not underscored* by the same line *are* significantly different.

2. Any two means *underscored* by the same line are *not* significantly different.

3. The means are arranged in ascending order from left to right.

4. The level of significance employed in applying the Kramer's test is 0.05 level.

From Table 5.28, it can be seen that the differences in the knowledge of nutrition between M_4 and M_3 and M_2 and M_1 are not statistically significant and the other mean differences viz., M_4 and M_2, M_4 and M_1, M_3 and M_2 and M_3 and M_1 are statistically significant.

Based on these results, it may be concluded that the respondents with family size of less than 4 members possess more knowledge than the other two groups. This suggests that as the family size of the respondent increases, his level of knowledge of nutrition decreases, that means, there is an inverse relationship between the sizc of the family and the level of knowledge of nutrition.

Experience and Knowledge of Nutrition

Length of service is reported to be one of the significant variables which can influence the level of knowledge of the instructors. Therefore, the total sample of 600 is divided into two groups on the basis of experience as instructors, namely, experienced (more than one year) and inexperienced (less than one year). To test the null hypothesis, 't' test was employed. Table 5.29 gives the means, SDs and the result of 't' test.

Table 5.29 : Experience-wise Differences in Knowledge of Nutrition

Experience Group	*N*	*M*	*SD*	*'t' value*
Experienced	306	34.7386	6.7226	
				3.5273**
Inexperienced	294	32.7381	7.1516	

** indicates significant at 0.01 level

A cursory glance of the above Table reveals that the calculated 't' value is significant beyond 0.01 level. Hence, the null hypothesis, is rejected. If we observe the means scores of the two groups, it is evident that the experienced instructors obtained higher mean score than inexperienced. It may be concluded that the experience of the instructor has influence on the level of knowledge of nutrition.

Reading Newspapers and Knowledge of Nutrition

Exposure to mass media is one of the important variables influencing the behaviour of individuals. It is a vital factor in bringing about modernization. Newspaper plays a significant role in the creation of a well informed citizen by disseminating news and views on diverse matters. Newspapers are an important means of education (Pavalkar et al., 1978). In recent years WHO, FAO and UNICEF have used newspapers in a variety of ways to promote nutritional status. To study the definite impact of newspapers in the acquisition of knowledge of nutrition among adult education instructors it is included in the present study. Of the total instructors, 388 are newspapers readers.

Table 5.30 : Readers and Non-Readers of Newspapers and Differences in Knowledge of Nutrition

Readers of Newspapers	*N*	*M*	*SD*	*'t' value*
Readers	388	34.2628	6.8344	2.3586*
Non-Readers	212	32.8349	7.2239	

** indicates significant at 0.05 level

The entries in Table 5.30 shows that the calculated 't' value is significant at 0.05 level of probability which demonstrates that reading newspapers and knowledge of nutrition are significantly related. This indicates that the readers of newspapers possess more knowledge of nutrition. Hence, the null hypothesis is rejected.

Listening to Radio and Knowledge of Nutrition

Radio, as a media is specially important due to its capacity to reach over great geographical distance and convey information to people. Radio is a powerful means to educate as well as entertain the rural people. According to Chanda Committee Report, primary importance should be given to rural broadcast to make the country self-sufficient in agricultural production, to improve health and nutritional status and hygiene and to give impetus to family planning. UNESCO has shown conclusive evidence that Radio has made significant contribution to the cause of education in many countries, developed as well as developing. A majority of the instructors (437) are listeners. To find out the impact on the acquisition of knowledge of nutrition, the data relating to listeners and non-listeners are presented in Table 5.31.

Table 5.31 : Listerners and Non-listeners of Radio and Differences in Knowledge of Nutrition

Radio Listening	*N*	*M*	*SD*	*'t' value*
Listeners	437	36.2540	6.8436	2.7792**
Non-listeners	163	32.4295	7.2653	

** indicates significant at 0.01 level

From the above Table, it is clear that the obtained 't' value (t = 2.7792) is significant beyond the 0.01 level of probability, indicating a strong influence of the independent variable on dependent variable. Radio stations in Andhra Pradesh broadcast items pertaining to knowledge of nutrition. Respondents who listened to Radio might have acquired more knowledge of nutrition.

Hence, the null hypothesis, namely, that 'there would not be significant influence of Radio on knowledge of nutrition', is rejected.

Viewing Films and Knowledge of Nutrition

India has emerged as a top producer of feature films in the world, producing on an average more than one picture per day. The role of films in social development has been increasingly emphasized since Independence. Hence, as a mass communication medium for bringing about the desired economic and social change in the country, the film can exert a far greater influence on the people than perhaps any other media. Apart from its continued and growing popularity, the film is also far more effective medium of communications than other media like Newspapers and Radio. The role of films as a source of entertainment has long been recognised. Its use as a means of education is of relatively recent origin. Films play a great role in educating the people and the memory will be everlasting and it will be more appealing to the people of all ages. Data on the distribution of film viewers and non-viewers are presented in Table 5.32.

Table 5.32 : Viewers and Non-viewers of Films and Differences in Knowledge of Nutrition

Film Viewing	*N*	*M*	*SD*	*'t' value*
Viewers	526	33.9202	6.9453	1.4499^{NS}
Non-viewers	74	32.6081	7.3352	

NS : indicates not significant.

It is seen from the Table 5.32, that the 't' value calculated is not significant even at 0.05 level of probability. This means, there is no significant influence of films on the level of knowledge of nutrition. It may be due to the fact that the news reels viewed by the audience may not have adequate content coverage and, hence, no difference between viewers and non-viewers. Therefore, the null hypothesis, namely, that 'there would not be significant influence of films on knowledge of nutrition', is retained.

Viewing Filmshows and Knowledge of Nutrition

Screening filmshows by various extension agencies has become quite common in rural areas. Filmshows are now very popular in rural areas. Filmshows on agriculture, health, nutrition and family planning are screened. They are.educative and provide knowledge. So far no attempt has been made to assess the impact of filmshows on the acquisition of knowledge of nutrition among adult education instructors. Data reveal that only about 203 respondents view filmshows. Table 5.33 explains as to whether viewing of filmshows has any impact on the knowledge of nutrition.

Table 5.33 : Viewers and Non-viewers of Filmshows and Differences in Knowledge of Nutrition

Viewing of filmshows	*N*	*M*	*SD*	*'t' value*
Viewes of filmshows	203	34.3399	6.6442	1.4923^{NS}
Non-viewers	397	33.4609	7.1685	

NS : indicates not significant.

A perusal of the above Table reveals that the obtained 't' value is not significant. It is evident that the filmshows have no effect on the level of knowledge of instructors, probably due to inadequate frequency of the projection of these films and lack of proper motivation among the adult education instructors to view the films. Therefore, the null hypothesis, is retained.

Viewing Television and Knowledge of Nutrition

Television has been rendering useful information service for nearly five decades and had laid a strong claim to be the most popular medium of mass communication particularly in the developed countries. India launched Television in 1959 on a small scale. The impact of Television on instructions in agriculture is reported to be tremendous. Of late, from 1980's, T.V. rely centres are being set up in different parts of the country and Educational Television Programmes (ETV) are launched on different subjects which are of great interest and need-based for both rural and urban masses. There are no large scale studies to assess the impact of T.V. on the acquisition of knowledge of nutrition in developing countries. It is of significance to assess the impact of T.V. on the acquisition of knowledge of nutrition because of rapid expansion of T.V. network in India. Table 5.34 shows the distribution of T.V. viewers and non-viewers. about 30.83 per cent of the respondents are reported to have seen T.V. programmes. It is very interesting to note that majority of the projects surveyed have community T.V. centres.

As seen from Table 5.34, the calculated 't' value is not significant even at 0.05 level of probability. This may be due to less frequency of viewing T.V. programmes and due to less coverage of content over the programmes on nutrition knowledge. Therefore, the null hypothesis is retained.

Table 5.34 : Viewers and Non-viewers of T.V. and Differences in Knowledge of Nutrition

Viewing of T.V.	*N*	*M*	*SD*	*'t' value*
Viewers	185	34.4973	6.7784	1.7581^{NS}
Non-viewers	415	33.4289	7.0829	

** indicates significant at 0.01 level

The next part deals with the influence of independent variables on attitude towards nutrition.

Attitudes Toward Nutrition

Attitude denotes inner feeling of a person. In other words, attitudes are personal dispositions which impel individuals to react to some object or situations. Attitude is probably the most important element of human behaviour. Obviously, it is difficult to expect the desired change in the action of an individual without a concomitant change in his/her thought (Sinha, 1972). "A knowledge of the attitudes of an individual helps a great deal in predicting, other things being equal, how he will act in a given situation" (Roy et al., 1968). There are long established traditional patterns of behaviour and complex problems of socio-economic, demographic, health and nutrition which are interwoven with attitudes and which support them and make them difficult to change. Hence, attitudes involve an emotional component. This is why when an attitude is formed, it becomes resistant to change, it does not generally respond to new facts. An attitude involve beliefs as well as evaluations.

Attitudes are not inherited and innate. They are learned and acquired in the course of experience. Some of them may be acquired from others but in any case they are learned. Attitudes are more or less permanent. But in the course of experience they may undergo change (Bhatia, 1976).

In this part, the influence of socio-economic and demographic factors on the attitudes toward nutrition are examined by means of 't' test, analysis of variance and Kramer's multiple range test. Each of the independent variable is considered separately to test the hypothesis.

Age and Attitudes Toward Nutrition

Traditions, interest, attitudes, etc., all become more fixed with age and they do not change as frequently as adolescents or youth (Murthy, 1981). Many of the nutritional attitudes are affected by age. At times age may be conducive to certain nutritional attitudes and in some cases it may not be so. Hence age determines the pattern of behaviour among members of the family. It is hypothesized that age as demographic variable may influence various nutritional attitudes. The influence of age on attitudes toward nutrition is presented in Table 5.35.

Table 5.35 : Differences in Attitudes Toward Nutrition : Age-wise Analysis

Age group	*N*	*M*	*SD*
Less than 20	139	114.6691	15.4307
21 – 25	161	119.1925	15.2036
26 – 30	115	121.1217	14.3388
More than 30	185	119.4000	15.4371

The trend of the mean scores indicates that the instructors in the age-group 26–30 are possessing relatively more favourable attitude towards nutrition than others. Whereas the instructors less than 20 years age-group are possessing little less favourable attitude. The summary of the analysis of variance shown below indicates whether these differences are significant.

It is clear from the Table 5.36, that the differences in attitudes among different age groups is highly significant. Hence, the null hypothesis that 'there would not be significant influence of age on attitudes towards nutrition', is rejected.

Table 5.36 : Summary of ANOVA of Attitudes Toward Nutrition of Different Age-groups

Source of Variance	*df*	*Sum of squares*	*Mean of squares*	*'F'*
Between groups	3	3053.0	1017.667	4.3938**
Within groups	596	138043.0	231.6158	
Total	**599**	**141096.0**		

**indicates significant at 0.01 level

To find out the age-group of instructors which differed significantly from the others in the extent of their attitudes towards nutrition, Kramer's multiple range test was employed. The results are presented in Table 5.37.

The results of the Kramer's test presented in the Table 5.37

Table 5.37 : Results of Kramer's Test Applied to Find the Significance of the Difference Among the Mean Attitude Scores of Instructors Classified According to their Age

	Less than 20 years M_1	*21–25* M_2	*More than 30 years* M_4	*26–30* M_3
N	139	161	185	115
M	114.6691	119.1925	119.4000	121.1217

Note : 1. Any two means *not underscored* by the same line *are* significantly different.

2. Any two means *underscored* by the same line are *not* significantly different.

3. The means are arranged in ascending order from left to right.

4. The level of significance employed in applying the Kramer's test is 0.05 level.

reveals that the instructors in less than 20 years age-group differed significantly from all the other three age groups. That means the instructors in younger age-group are having low attitude towards nutrition. It may be due to immaturity and less exposure to the community.

Sex and Attitudes Toward Nutrition

Sex is a biologically ascribed characteristic. To a considerable extent sex determines the pattern of behaviour among members of the family. Indian culture expects women to be submissive and obedient in the family. This situation makes them develop a set of attitudes. So far no attempt has been made to see the relationship between sex roles and nutritional attitudes among adult education instructors. The review presented in Chapter 2 did not show conclusive evidence to build a theory about the relationship between sex and attitudes toward nutrition. To know the influence of sex on attitudes toward nutrition, the attitudes classified on the basis of sex are presented in the Table 5.38.

Table 5.38 : Differences in Attitudes Toward Nutrition : Sex-wise Analysis

Sex Group	*N*	*M*	*SD*	*'t' value*
Male	329	118.079	14.0124	0.8643^{NS}
Female	271	119.1845	16.7813	

NS : indicates not significant

From the Table 5.38, it is evident that the difference between male and female instructors' mean scores is not significant, as the 't' value calculated is less than the Table value. Therefore, we can conclude that sex of the instructors has no influence on the attitudes towards nutrition and hence, the null hypothesis that 'there would not be significant influence of sex on attitude towards nutrition', is retained.

Annual Income and Attitudes toward Nutrition

Income is strongly associated with many socio, economic and demographic factors. In order to understand the relationship between family annual income and the attitudes toward nutrition, the total sample has been divided into four groups on the basis of their annual income and the data are presented in the Table 5.39.

Table 5.39 : Differences in Attitudes Toward Nutrition : Income-wise Analysis

Income group	*N*	*M*	*SD*
Less than 2,500	115	118.6783	15.8765
2,501 – 3,500	166	115.4398	13.6948
3,501 – 4,500	189	119.4392	16.3756
Above 4,500	130	121.2462	14.5687

An observation of the mean scores of the Table reveals that the instructors with higher income possess more favourable attitude towards nutrition than the other three income groups. The summary of the analysis of variance shown below discloses whether these differences are significant.

It divulges from Table 5.40 that the difference in attitudes of instructors of different income groups is significant, as the obtained 'F' value is significant at 0.01 level of probability. Therefore, the null hypothesis, is rejected.

Table 5.40 : Summary of ANOVA of Attitude Scores of Different Income Groups

Source of Variance	*df*	*Sum of squares*	*Mean of squares*	*'F'*
Between groups	3	2701	900.3333	3.8773**
Within groups	596	138395	232.2064	
Total	**599**	**141096**		

**indicates significant at 0.01 level

However, the analysis was further carried on to test the significant difference between the different sets of income groups. Kramer's multiple range test was employed.

It is evident from Table 5.41 that the instructors in the income range of Rs. 2,501–3,500 obtained a low mean score of 115.4398 and had low attitude towards nutrition and differed significantly from the instructors whose annual income was Rs. 3,501–4,500 and more than Rs. 4,500.

Table 5.41 : Results of Kramer's Test Applied to Find the Significance of the Difference Among the Mean Knowledge Scores of Instructors Classified According to their Family Income

	2,501–3,500 M_2	*Less than 2,500* M_1	*3,501–4,500* M_3	*Above 4,500* M_4
N	166	115	189	130
M	115.4398	118.6783	119.4392	121.2462

Note : 1. Any two means *not underscored* by the same line *are* significantly different.

2. Any two means *underscored* by the same line are *not* significantly different.

3. The means are arranged in ascending order from left to right.

4. The level of significance employed in applying the Kramer's test is 0.05 level.

Caste and Attitudes Towards Nutrition

Caste is an ascribed status by birth. The influence of caste in Indian society is very powerful. The caste determines the style of life, belief–systems, instructions and also affects the treatment which an individual receives from others. Today, caste distinctions in certain spheres of social life are seen clearly than ever before and there is evidence to suggest that caste identifications have assumed new meaningful quality in numerous spheres of life (Srinivasa, 1962, 1965; Gould, 1963; Radolph, 1967). Members of different castes were upto a point expected to behave differently and have different values and ideals (Beteille, 1971). High castes as well as low reveal the effects of their status in attitudes as well as in their values, beliefs and behaviour (Cash, 1954; Smith, 1963; and Mannoni, 1964). The influence of caste over attitudes toward nutrition is presented in Table 5.42.

A perusal of the mean scores of Table 5.42 indicates that there is an apparent difference in attitudes among the different caste groups. To see whether they differ significantly, analysis of variance technique was employed. The summary of analysis of variance is given in Table 5.43.

Table 5.42 : Differences in Attitudes Toward Nutrition : Caste-wise Analysis

Caste group	*N*	*M*	*SD*
Forward Caste	161	118.087	16.4768
Backward Caste	248	119.3065	15.0481
Scheduled Caste/ Scheduled Tribe	191	118.0471	14.6521

Table 5.43 : Summary of ANOVA of Attitude Scores of Instructors of Different Caste-groups

Source of Variance	*df*	*Sum of squares*	*Mean of squares*	*'F'*
Between groups	2	224	112	0.4746^{NS}
Within groups	597	140872	235.9665	
Total	**599**	**141096**		

NS : indicates not significant

As the 'F' ratio calculated is not significant even at 0.05 level of probability for 2 and 597 degrees of freedom, the null hypothesis that, 'there would not be significant influence of caste on attitudes toward nutrition', is retained. In other words, we can conclude that caste has no bearing on attitudes of instructors toward nutrition.

Religion and Attitudes Toward Nutrition

The economic, political and other attitudes are affected by religious affiliation. Religion influences moral, ethical and marital views (Childs, 1965). Religion also influences the pattern of food habits and beliefs to some extent which in turn influences the behaviour of the people. Table 5.44 presents attitude scores of different religious groups.

The mean scores show a negligible variations among the three groups with regard to their attitudes toward nutrition. Christians appeared to have a more favourable tendency towards nutrition. However, ANOVA technique was employed to see whether there exists any significant difference among the three groups.

Table 5.44 : Differences in Attitudes Toward Nutrition : Religion-wise Analysis

Religion group	*N*	*M*	*SD*
Hindus	527	118.4345	15.4123
Muslims	40	118.55	16.1012
Christians	33	120.9091	12.7359

A glance through Table 5.45 points out that religion has no effect on the attitudes of instructors toward nutrition, as the calculated 'F' value is not significant. Therefore, the null hypothesis, is retained. In other words, instructors belonging to different religions do not differ significantly in their attitude towards nutrition.

Table 5.45 : Summary of ANOVA of Attitude Scores of Instructors of Different Religions

Source of Variance	*df*	*Sum of squares*	*Mean of squares*	*'F'*
Between groups	2	190	95	0.4025^{NS}
Within groups	597	140906	236.0235	
Total	**599**	**141096**		

NS : indicates not significant

Marital Status and Attitudes Toward Nutrition

So far no attempt has been made to study the type of relationship between marital status and attitudes toward nutrition among adult education instructors. Those who entered into married life may possess one set of attitudes and the unmarried may possess another set of attitudes. Attitudinal differences between married and unmarried instructors are presented in Table 5.46.

The data clearly show that the difference in the mean scores between married and unmarried instructors is statistically significant. It can be concluded that married instructors possess more favourable attitude towards nutrition than unmarried instructors. The family life of the married might have fostered positive attitude towards nutrition.

Table 5.46 : Differences in Attitudes Toward Nutrition : Marital Status-wise Analysis

Marital Status	*N*	*M*	*SD*	*'t' value*
Married	317	119.9748	15.3635	2.3737*
Unmarried	283	117.0141	15.1508	

* indicates significant at 0.05 level

Hence, the null hypothesis, namely, that 'there would not be significant influence of marital status on attitudes toward nutrition', is rejected.

Occupation and Attitudes toward Nutrition

Persons belonging to different occupations may possess different sets of attitudes. Their occupation may make them to form such attitudes. So far, no attempt has been made to study the nutritional attitudes of adult education instructors. The differences in attitudes based on occupation are presented in Table 5.47.

Table 5.47 : Occupation-wise Differences in Attitudes Toward Nutrition

Occupation Group	*N*	*M*	*SD*
Agriculture	206	116.5728	15.0039
Caste Occupants	114	117.4649	14.5459
Self-employment/Business	123	121.4472	15.9416
Others	157	119.7707	15.3801

It is evident from Table 5.47 that the instructors who are self-employed/business do possess more favourable attitude towards nutrition than the other three groups. Differences between the means indicate that there exists significant difference. The summary of analysis of variance presented below reveals the same.

If is seen from the Table 5.48 that there is significant difference in attitudes among different occupational groups as the 'F' value is significant at 0.05 level of probability. It is considered that occupation of the instructor is a potential factor influencing the attitudes toward nutrition. It is also evident that the instructors engaged in self-

Table 5.48 : Summary of ANOVA of Attitude Scores of Instructors with Different Occupations

Source of Variance	*df*	*Sum of squares*	*Mean of squares*	*'F'*
Between groups	3	2205	735	3.1539*
Within groups	596	138891	233.0386	
Total	**599**	**141096**		

* indicates significant at 0.05 level

employment/business appeared to have more favourable attitude towards nutrition than other groups. The reasons are quite obvious. Hence, the null hypothesis, is rejected.

However, to know the groups whose difference is significant, Kramer's multiple range test was employed. The results are presented in the Table 5.49.

Table 5.49 : Results of Kramer's Test Applied to Find the Significance of the Difference Among the Mean Attitude Scores of Instructors Classified According to their Occupations

	Agriculture M_1	*Caste occupants* M_2	*Others* M_4	*Self-employed/ Business* M_3
N	206	114	157	123
M	116.5728	117.4649	119.7707	121.4472

Note : 1. Any two means *not underscored* by the same line *are* significantly different.

2. Any two means *underscored* by the same line are *not* significantly different.

3. The means are arranged in ascending order from left to right.

4. The level of significance employed in applying the Kramer's test is 0.05 level.

It is clear from the Table 5.49 that the instructors whose basic occupation is agriculture differed significantly from people engaged in business/self-employment. The probable reason may be that the instructors who are self-employed/business might have several contracts and interaction with the people and this in turn might have helped them to have a high favourable attitude towards nutrition.

Educational Status and Attitudes Toward Nutrition

Education is strongly associated with attitudes as attitudes are acquired beliefs. Education felicitates more learning opportunities to the individuals. Learning helps the individual to develop favourable tendencies towards concepts. Based on the educational qualifications of the instructors, they are classified into four groups and the data are presented in the Table 5.50.

Table 5.50 : Differences in Attitudes Toward Nutrition : Education-wise Analysis

Education Qualification	*N*	*M*	*SD*
8 years of schooling	63	111.4127	14.6338
10 years of schooling	348	116.546	15.3288
12 years of schooling	143	123.8392	14.2748
Above 12 years of schooling	46	127.413	9.8634

An observation of the above Table indicates an increasing trend of mean scores of attitudes toward nutrition. Higher the educational qualification, higher is the mean score of attitudes. The summary of analysis of variance shown in Table 5.51 discloses whether these differences are significant.

Table 5.51 : Summary of ANOVA of Attitude Scores of Instructors with Varied Educational Qualifications

Source of Variance	*df*	*Sum of squares*	*Mean of squares*	*'F'*
Between groups	3	12220	4073.333	18.8375**
Within groups	596	128876	216.235	
Total	**599**	**141096**		

** indicates significant at 0.01 level

As the calculated 'F' value is far higher than the Table value for 3, 596 df, at 0.01 level of probability, the null hypothesis, is rejected. Further it can be concluded that the instructors with higher educational qualification possess more favourable attitude towards nutrition than the instructors with low education background.

However, to identify the groups which differ significantly Kramer's multiple range test is employed and the results are presented in Table 5.52.

Table 5.52 : Results of Kramer's Test Applied to Find the Significance of the Difference Among the Mean Attitude Scores of Instructors with Different Educational Qualifications

	8 years of schooling *Group M_1*	*10 years of schooling* *Group M_2*	*12 years of schooling* *Group M_3*	*Above 12 years of schooling* *Group M_4*
N	63	348	143	46
M	111.4127	116.546	123.8392	127.413

Note : 1. Any two means *not underscored* by the same line *are* significantly different.

2. Any two means *underscored* by the same line are *not* significantly different.

3. The means are arranged in ascending order from left to right.

4. The level of significance employed in applying the Kramer's test is 0.05 level.

From Table 5.52, it can be seen that the difference in the attitudes toward nutrition between groups M_3 and M_4 is not statistically significant whereas the mean differences between groups M_1 and M_2, M_1 and M_3, M_1 and M_4, M_2 and M_4 and M_2 and M_3 are statistically significant. There is attitudinal difference between the two group possessing 8 or 10 years of schooling and 12 or above 12 years of schooling. Therefore, the people to be preferred for appointment as adult education instructors should atleast possess more than 10 years of schooling.

Family Type and Attitudes Toward Nutrition

The family is the most universal and permanent institution of mankind. But today, radical changes are found in every sphere of life—political, economical, social and cultural. The changes in socio-economic conditions of people are also reflected in the institution of the family. With family structure undergoing profound modification, it is of great interest to determine whether family type in India still exerts an influence on individual decisions and behaviour. The review presented did not explain clear-cut relationship between family type and attitudes toward nutrition. Whether family type in India influence nutritional attitudes is shown in the Table 5.53.

Table 5.53 : Differences in Attitudes Toward Nutrition Between Joint and Nuclear Families

Family Type	*N*	*M*	*SD*	*'t' value*
Joint	413	117.5811	14.8382	2.3031*
Nuclear	187	120.7808	16.1623	

* indicates significant at 0.05 level

A cursory glance through the above Table reveals that the obtained 't' value (t = 2.3031) is significant beyond 0.05 level of probability. It is clear that there is a significant difference in the attitudes toward nutrition between the instructors who are living in nuclear families and joint families. On the basis of the mean scores, it may be concluded that the respondents living in nuclear families possess more favourable attitudes towards nutrition than those who live in joint families. The reason is that the members in the nuclear families will have more interaction and have value for the food they are taking. Hence, the null hypothesis that 'the influence of the type of the family on the attitudes toward nutrition is not significant', is rejected.

Family Size and Attitudes Toward Nutrition

There are no large scale studies explaining the influence of family size on attitudes toward nutrition among adult education instructors. Hence, it is of great interest to know as to how the size of the family of the respondents influence their nutritional attitude. The mean scores, standard deviations and number of subjects in each of the four groups are presented in the Table 5.54.

Table 5.54 : Differences in Attitudes toward Nutrition : Family Size-wise Analysis

Group	*N*	*M*	*SD*
Less than 4	174	121.2529	15.3355
5 – 6	193	118.7928	15.0494
7 – 8	125	116.12	14.2692
More than 8	108	116.7315	16.2832

The mean scores of the above Table reveal that instructors having family size of less than four members are possessing favourable tendency towards nutrition than instructors having family size of more than eight members. However, the ANOVA technique was employed to see whether there exist any significant difference among the mean scores. The results are presented in the Table 5.55.

Table 5.55 : Summary of ANOVA of Attitudes Scores of Instructors of Different Family Sizes

Source of Variance	*df*	*Sum of squares*	*Mean of squares*	*'F'*
Between groups	3	2377	792.3333	3.4042*
Within groups	596	138719	232.75	
Total	**599**	**141096**		

* indicates significant at 0.05 level

As can be seen from the above Table, the calculated 'F' value is significant and denotes the significant differences in attitudes among different family size groups. Hence, the null hypothesis, is rejected.

As the calculated 'F' value is found to be significant, to know the two groups which differed significantly, Kramer's multiple range test was employed. The results are presented in Table 5.56.

Based on the results shown in Table 5.56, it may be concluded that the respondents with minimum family size possess more favourable attitude than the respondents with maximum family size. This

Table 5.56 : Results of Kramer's Test Applied to Find the Significance of the Difference Among the Mean Attitude Scores of Instructors of Different Family Sizes

	7 – 8 Members M_3	*Above 8 members* M_4	*5 – 6 Members* M_2	*Less than 4 Members* M_1
N	125	108	193	174
M	116.12	116.7315	118.7928	121.2529

Note : 1. Any two means *not underscored* by the same line *are* significantly different.

2. Any two means *underscored* by the same line are *not* significantly different.

3. The means are arranged in ascending order from left to right.

4. The level of significance employed in applying the Kramer's test is 0.05 level.

suggests that as the family size of the respondents increases their attitude towards nutrition gets reduced.

Experience and Attitudes Towards Nutrition

Experience is reported to be one of the significant variables which can influence the attitudes toward nutrition. 't' test was employed to know whether experience influences attitudes or not. Table 5.57 gives the results of the 't' test.

Table 5.57 : Experience-wise Differences in Attitudes Toward Nutrition

Group	*N*	*M*	*SD*	*'t' value*
Experienced (more than one year)	306	118.7908	15.7951	0.3468^{NS}
Inexperienced (less than one year)	294	118.3571	14.8376	

NS : indicates not significant

A perusal of Table 5.57 reveals that experience has not influenced the attitudes of the respondents toward nutrition. Hence, the null hypothesis, is retained.

Reading Newspapers and Attitude Towards Nutrition

There are several ways in which the communication source can influence the decision making process at individual level. It has a specific role to play in the promotion of nutrition programmes among the public. Expert opinion varies concerning the power of mass media to affect the attitudes, beliefs and behaviour of human beings (Wilder, 1973). So far, newspapers are untapped source for purposes of nutrition education. The attitudinal differences between Readers and Non-Readers of newspapers are presented in Table 5.58.

Table 5.58 : Readers and Non-Readers of Newspapers and Differences in Attitude Towards Nutrition

Readers of Newspapers	*N*	*M*	*SD*	*'t' value*
Readers	388	119.1856	15.2709	1.3117^{NS}
Non-Readers	212	117.4670	15.3894	

NS : indicates not significant

A reference to Table 5.58 clearly shows that the difference between means of those who read newspapers and those who do not read is not significant. It can be inferred that newspapers reading has no influence on attitude towards nutrition among adult education instructors. Hence, the null hypothesis, is retained.

Listening to Radio and Attitude Towards Nutrition

The role of radio as a teaching medium has been widely recognised in many countries. Radio broadcasts have been in use in India also. The most popular medium of mass communication in rural areas where majority of inhabitants are illiterates is radio. Most of the uneducated can be educated through radio programmes. Radio can be the most important link between knowledgeable and the ignorant (Bhattacharya, 1976). Hence, radio, as a source of mass media may be justified as an important contributor to attitudinal change (Yadav, 1975). Table 5.59 explains as to whether listening to radio on nutrition matters has any impact on the attitudes toward nutrition.

Table 5.59 : Listeners and Non-Listeners of Radio and Differences in Attitude Towards Nutrition

Listening to Radio	*N*	*M*	*SD*	*'t' value*
Listeners	437	119.3455	15.2834	2.0133*
Non-listeners	163	116.5115	15.2836	

* indicates significant at 0.05 level

As can be known from Table 5.59, the obtained 't' value (t = 2.01333) is significant at 0.05 level of probability. This indicates that listeners of radio possess more favourable attitude towards nutrition than non-listeners. Hence, the null hypothesis, namely, that 'there would not be significant influence of radio on attitudes toward nutrition', is rejected.

Viewing Films and Attitude Towards Nutrition

Films are very popular with rural and urban masses. Cinema is considered to be relatively more effective medium because of the visibility of the objects/incidents on the screen. Films have tremendous impact on the masses. This medium can be suitably commissioned to motivate people in the attitudinal change in all walks of life. If blended with a social message, a film can have an immediate impact on the spectators (Bhattacharya, 1976). Data on the distribution of film viewers and non-viewers and their attitudes are presented in Table 5.60.

Table 5.60 : Viewers and Non-viewers of Films and Differences in Attitude Towards Nutrition

Film Viewing	*N*	*M*	*SD*	*'t' value*
Viewers	526	118.8783	15.3677	1.3077^{NS}
Non-viewers	74	116.446	14.9269	

NS : indicates not significant

A cursory glance through Table 5.60 indicates that the calculated 't' value is not significant even at 0.05 level of probability. This means, there is no significant influence of films on attitude towards nutrition. It may be due to the disinterest in viewing news-reels by the audience or lack of presentation of such content adequately through news-reels. Hence, the null hypothesis is retained.

Viewing Filmshows—Attitude Towards Nutrition

Just like films, filmshows may be effective to some degree in changing some attitudes. Filmshows implant or strengthen attitudes. Hence, filmshows may also have definite impact on the nutritional attitudes. Table 5.61 explains as to whether viewing of filmshows has any impact on the attitude towards nutrition.

Table 5.61 : Viewers and Non-viewers of Filmshows and Differences in Attitude Towards Nutrition

Viewing of Filmshows	*N*	*M*	*SD*	*'t' value*
Viewers of filmshows	203	119.1626	14.7708	0.6795^{NS}
Non-viewers	397	118.2796	15.6071	

NS : indicates not significant

The entries in Table 5.61 show that the difference in the mean scores of attitudes between viewers and non-viewers of filmshows is not significant. Hence, the null hypothesis, is retained. It is evident that the filmshows have no effect on the attitude towards nutrition among adult education instructors. This may be due to less frequency of projection of the filmshows related to nutrition and health and also lack of proper motivation among the instructors to view the filmshows even if projected.

Viewing Television and Attitude Towards Nutrition

Television as one of the mass media of communication has unique features and has a marked advantage over other mass contact methods. It is an instantaneous audio and visual media. It provides words with pictures of live situations and sound effect like other movies. It is also called the magic media of mass communication (Swamy, et al., 1978). Television is yet to be tried out on a mass scale in Indian villages for motivational changes. It is hypothesized that educational programmes of Television may change time-hallowed attitudes of rural masses on such matters as health, nutrition, family planning and agriculture. Table 5.62 shows the distribution of attitudes of Television viewers and non-viewers.

Table 5.62 : Viewers and Non-viewers of Television and Differences in Attitude Towards Nutrition

Viewing of Television	*N*	*M*	*SD*	*'t' value*
Viewers	185	119.1459	15.6127	0.5995^{NS}
Non-viewers	415	118.3253	15.2027	

NS : indicates not significant

A perusal of Table 5.62 indicates that the obtained 't' value is not significant even at 0.05 level of probability. The reasons may be (1) only very few people, i.e., less than 1/3 of the total sample are exposed to Television programmes, (2) less frequency of viewing Television programmes and (3) lack of attention over the programmes on nutrition in particular. Therefore, the null hypothesis that 'there would not be significant influence of Television on attitude towards nutrition', is retained.

The influence of independent variables on practices of nutrition is detailed in the next part.

Practices of Nutrition

The notion of selection is always at work in the acceptance and rejection of innovations. Hence, some of the innovations are bitterly resisted and others are welcomed. For some, success comes early, for others it may come lately. Many common socio-economic and socio-cultural variables have been found to be associated with the adoption of different types of improved technologies like improved agricultural practices, improved health innovations and improved family planning methods. But the pattern and nature of adoption of various innovations have been observed to vary from one group to another, the extent of variation depending upon the intensity of socio-cultural differences which exist between the groups (Mujumdar et al., 1972). Some innovations may be easily and readily accepted, others might meet with resistance or indifference. The successful adoption of innovation depends partly upon the nature of innovations itself and partly on the social and cultural character of the people among whom it is introduced and consequently different social systems may react differently to the same innovation (Gopalan et al., 1971). Adoption of agricultural innovations or any other innovation depend upon various factors. Not only in India but even in the advanced countries of the West, adoption involves decision making on the part of the individual. The decision depends not only on the economic advantages occurring from adoption but also depends upon the social setting in which the individual is placed. In India, caste, type and size of the family assume a special importance in this field. The educational factor is important as it makes the people see the advantages following from the adoption of an improved practice. Health innovations require less economic investment than agriculture. But the adoption of health innovations are affected by socio, economic and demographic factors (Sachchidanand, 1972). Also, values and attitudes of the people do influence their decisions for or against the adoption of an innovation. The influence of socio, economic and demographic factors on the practices of nutrition is presented in this part.

Age and Practices of Nutrition

Age is a personal factor. Age plays a significant role in the matter of behaviour. One might expect age to be important factor in the adoption of recommended practices. All people, irrespective of social milieu in which they have been brought up, are receptive to new ideas and things at a certain age level. Before they reach that age level, they are not in a position to take independent decisions and after that age they are resistant to change. Receptivity or resistance to change also depends upon the psychological make-up of persons. Several studies of adoption practices have considered age as an important factor in the adoption of innovations. The presumption is that it is at a comparatively young age that people are more receptive to new ideas and practices. At an advanced age people find it difficult to change from age-old practices (Sachchidananda, 1972).

The young people are supposed to be radical and progressive and as such interested in new practices. On the other hand, the old are conservative and reluctant to adopt new improved practices. It is necessary to quantify the impact of age on nutrition practices. Table 5.63 presents the effect of age on nutritional practices.

An observation of the mean scores indicates that instructors in the age group of above 30 years are highly practicing group than the other three groups. However, ANOVA technique was employed to see whether there exists any significant difference among four groups.

Table 5.63 : Differences in Practices of Nutrition : Age-wise Analysis

Age group in years	*N*	*M*	*SD*
Less than 20	139	21.1943	4.5847
21 – 25	161	20.85093	5.5563
26 – 30	115	21.0	5.2486
Above 30	185	21.4054	5.8136

Table 5.64 : Summary of ANOVA of Practice Scores of Instructors of Different Age Groups

Source of Variance	*df*	*Sum of squares*	*Mean of squares*	*'F'*
Between groups	3	29.125	9.7083	0.3342^{NS}
Within groups	596	17312.75	29.0482	
Total	**599**	**17341.875**		

NS : indicates not significant

As the 'F' ratio calculated is not significant even at 0.05 level of probability for 3, 596 degrees of freedom, the null hypothesis that 'there would not be significant influence of age on practices of nutrition', is retained.

Sex and Practices of Nutrition

The mean scores of male and female instructors and the corresponding standard deviations are presented in the following Table to see whether there exists significant difference between the two groups of instructors in their nutritional practices.

Table 5.65 : Differences in Practices of Nutrition : Sex-wise Analysis

Sex Group	*N*	*M*	*SD*	*'t' value*
Male	329	20.5623	5.0333	2.8358**
Female	271	21.8192	5.6894	

** indicates significant at 0.01 level

It is evident from the above Table that the difference between the mean scores pertaining to practices of nutrition of males and females is significant at 0.01 level of probability. It is also clear from the Table that female mean scores are high compared to males. It may be due to the fact that females are more concerned about cooking and family functions than males. Hence, females' practices scores are more. It is also customary in India, that women will look after cooking food and child rearing.

Therefore, the null hypothesis, that 'there would not be significant influence of sex on practices of nutrition', is rejected.

Annual Income and Practices of Nutrition

It is fact that economic status influences individual behaviour in different walks of life in different ways. The various studies conducted in different parts of the country reveal that the farmers of higher economic status are quick to adopt modern practices (Sachchidananda. 1972). Family income is found to be positively related to adoption of modern agricultural practices (Fliagel, 1957 and Frank, 1967). To investigate into this aspect, the instructors are classified into four categories on the basis of their annual income of the family and the differences in practices are presented in Table 5.66.

Table 5.66 : Difference in Practives of Nutrition : Income-wise Analysis

Income Group	*N*	*M*	*SD*
Less than 2,500	115	21.3836	6.0095
2,501 – 3,500	166	20.5843	4.8992
3,501 – 4,500	189	21.7302	5.3429
Above 4,500	130	20.7308	5.3086

It is clear from Table 5.66 that mean scores of the respondents belonging to less than 2,500 and 3,501–4,500 income groups are more than the people belonging to 2,501–3,500 and above 4,500 income groups. Analysis of variance technique was employed to test whether these differences are significant or not and the results are shown in the Table 5.67.

The results indicate that the calculated 'F' is not significant even at 0.05 level of probability. Therefore, the null hypothesis that 'there

Table 5.67 : Summary of ANOVA of Practice Scores of Instructors of Different Income Groups

Source of Variance	*df*	*Sum of squares*	*Mean of squares*	*'F'*
Between groups	3	145.5625	48.5208	1.6817^{NS}
Within groups	596	17196.31	28.8529	
Total	**599**	**17341.875**		

NS : indicates not significant

would not be significant influence of annual income on the practices of nutrition', is retained. In other words, we can conclude that it appears that income has no bearing on the practices of nutrition.

Caste and Practices of Nutrition

The Indian social system is inconceivable without caste. Caste influences all other aspects of life. It is one of the dominant themes in any discussion on economic development and growth. In some recent studies on adoption and diffusion, some light has been thrown on caste as a correlation of adoption of agriculture innovations (Santipriya Bose, 1961; Roy et al., 1968; and Sachchidananda, 1972). But there is dearth of knowledge on the relationship between caste and nutrition practices of adult education instructors. Caste-wise differences in nutritional practices are shown in the Table 5.68.

Table 5.68 : Differences in Practices of Nutrition : Caste-wise Analysis

Caste group	*N*	*M*	*SD*
Forward Caste	161	22.0	5.3254
Backward Caste	248	21.0605	5.0506
Scheduled Caste/ Scheduled Tribe	191	20.4869	5.7193

By observing the trend in the mean scores, it appears that the nutrition practices are low in the instructors belonging to Scheduled Caste/Scheduled Tribes whereas the practices of the Forward Caste respondents are very high. To know whether the difference between the three groups is significant, analysis of variance technique was employed and the results are presented in Table 5.69.

Table 5.69 : Summary of ANOVA of Practice Scores of Instructors of Different Caste Groups

Source of Variance	*df*	*Sum of squares*	*Mean of squares*	*'F'*
Between groups	2	202.0625	101.0313	3.5190*
Within groups	597	17139.81	28.7099	
Total	**599**	**17341.8725**		

* indicates significant at 0.05 level

It is evident from the above Table, that there is significant difference in practices among different caste groups, as the 'F' calculated is greater than 'F' table value. It is considered that caste of the instructor is a significant factor influencing the practices of nutrition. The probable reason for this is that most of the Scheduled Caste/Scheduled Tribes live below poverty line. Sometimes in few cases it is difficult to have atleast one meal per day. Their standard of living is low when compared to other caste people. Hence, the null hypothesis, is rejected.

However, to know the groups within which differences exists, Kramer's multiple range test was employed and the results are given in Table 5.70.

It is quite clear from Table 5.70 that the practices of instructors belonging to Scheduled Caste/Scheduled Tribes are significantly different from Forward Caste instructors.

Religion and Practices of Nutrition

In India, religion has a special significance as it is closely associated with food beliefs, customs, taboos which have a great impact on nutrition practices. The religion-wise differences in nutrition practices are presented in Table 5.71.

A cursory glance through Table 5.71 shows that Hindus appeared to have little more mean score than the other two religions. However, the ANOVA technique was employed to see whether there exists any significant difference among the three groups and the results are tabulated in Table 5.72.

Table 5.70 : Results of Kramer's Test Applied to Find the Significance of the Difference Among the Mean Practice Scores of Instructors of Different Caste Groups

	Scheduled Caste Scheduled Tribe M_3	*Backward Caste* M_2	*Forward Caste* M_1
N	191	248	161
M	20.4869	21.0605	22.0

Note : 1. Any two means *not underscored* by the same line *are* significantly different.

2. Any two means *underscored* by the same line are *not* significantly different.

3. The means are arranged in ascending order from left to right

4. The level of significance employed in applying the Kramer's test is 0.05 level.

Table 5.71 : Differences in Practices of Nutrition : Religion-wise Analysis

Religious group	*N*	*M*	*SD*
Hindus	527	21.2543	5.4595
Muslims	40	20.05	4.4212
Christians	33	20.4546	4.8685

Table 5.72 : Summary of ANOVA of Practice Scores of Instructors of Different Religions

Source of Variance	*df*	*Sum of squares*	*Mean of squares*	*'F'*
Between groups	2	69.8438	34.9219	1.2071^{NS}
Within groups	597	17272.03	28.9314	
Total	**599**	**17341.8738**		

NS : indicates not significant

As the 'F' value is not significant even at 0.05 level of probability for 2,597 degrees of freedom, the null hypothesis that 'there would not be significant influence of religion on practices of nutrition', is retained. Therefore, it can be concluded that religion appears to have no significant influence on practices of nutrition.

Marital Status and Practices of Nutrition

To test whether there is significant difference between the married and unmarried instructors in their practices, 't' test was employed. The mean scores and standard deviations of both the groups with the results of 't' test are shown in the Table 5.73.

Table 5.73 : Differences in Practices of Nutrition : Marital Status-wise Analysis

Marital Status	*N*	*M*	*SD*	*'t' value*
Married	317	21.4669	5.5847	1.6363^{NS}
Unmarried	283	20.7527	5.1062	

NS : indicates not significant.

The calculated 't' value is not significant. Therefore, the null hypothesis, is retained. Marital status has no bearing or influence on nutritional practices.

Occupation and Practices of Nutrition

The occupation of a person may influence the practices. So far, no attempt has been made to study as to how the main occupation of a person influences various nutrition practices among adult education instructors. Occupation-wise difference in nutritional practices of instructors find a place in Table 5.74.

Table 5.74 : Differences in Practices of Nutrition : Occupation-wise Analysis

Occupation group	*N*	*M*	*SD*
Agriculture	206	20.4563	5.1864
Caste Occupants	114	21.0526	5.2228
Self-employed/Business	123	22.0	5.6063
Others	157	21.3885	5.4289

The data in Table 5.74 show that the mean score of self-employed/business respondents is relatively more than the other occupational groups. Analysis of variance technique was employed to test whether there was any significant difference among the mean scores of the four groups and the results are shown in the Table 5.75.

Table 5.75 : Summary of ANOVA of Practice Scores of Instructors with Different Occupations

Source of Variance	*df*	*Sum of squares*	*Mean of squares*	*'F'*
Between groups	3	197.7813	65.9271	
				2.2919^{NS}
Within groups	596	17144.09	28.7653	
Total	**599**	**17341.8713**		

NS : indicates not significant

The 'F' ratio is far below the value required to be significant at 0.05 level of probability for 3, 596 degrees of freedom. It means that there is no significant influence of occupation on practices of nutrition and hence, the null hypothesis, is retained.

Educational Status and Practices of Nutrition

The sample of instructors are divided into four groups depending upon their educational qualifications. It is generally believed that higher the qualifications, higher will be the nutrition practices. The trend in the mean scores of nutritional practices in relation to educational level of the instructors are shown in Table 5.76.

Table 5.76 : Differences in Practices of Nutrition : Education-wise Analysis

Educational Qualifications	*N*	*M*	*SD*
8 years of schooling	63	17.8571	6.5897
10 years of schooling	348	20.7845	5.0403
12 years of schooling	143	22.6364	4.8625
Above 12 years of schooling	46	23.5435	4.8351

A perusal of the Table 5.76 indicates an increasing trend of mean scores of practices of nutrition with reference to educational level. Higher the qualification, higher is the mean score of practices. The summary of analysis of variance shown in Table 5.77 discloses whether these differences are significant.

Table 5.77 : Summary of ANOVA of Practice Scores of Instructors with Varied Educational Qualifications

Source of Variance	*df*	*Sum of squares*	*Mean of squares*	*'F'*
Between groups	3	1308.813	436.2709	16.2176**
Within groups	596	16033.06	26.9011	
Total	**599**	**17341.873**		

** indicates significant at 0.01 level

The calculated 'F' value denotes that there is significant difference in practices among different educational groups. Hence, the null hypothesis, is rejected.

As the calculated 'F' value is significant, to know the two groups which differed significantly, Kramer's multiple range test was employed. The results are presented in Table 5.78.

Table 5.78 : Results of Kramer's Test Applied to Find the Significance of the Difference Among the Mean Practice Scores of Instructors of Different Education Groups

	8 years of schooling M_1	*10 years of schooling* M_2	*12 years of schooling* M_3	*Above 12 years of schooling* M_4
N	63	348	143	46
M	17.8571	20.7845	22.6364	23.5435

Note : 1. Any two means *not underscored* by the same line *are* significantly different.

2. Any two means *underscored* by the same line are *not* significantly different.

3. The means are arranged in ascending order from left to right.

4. The level of significance employed in applying the Kramer's test is 0.05 level.

From Table 5.78, it is clear that there is no statistically significant difference in practices between the respondents having 12 years and above 12 years of schooling. But there is a difference between the respondents in other educational groups M_1 & M_2, M_1 & M_3, M_1 & M_4, M_2 & M_4 and M_2 & M_3.

Family Type and Practices of Nutrition

Old agrarian societies like that of India and China have been characterised as familistic. The entire social organisation and values and beliefs of people centre around these social institutions. Most of the families, especially in rural areas are joint or extended in composition. Most of the land-owning groups still live in extended and joint families while bulk of the agricultural labourers generally have nuclear families. The important feature of the structure of the traditional Indian society is the joint family. Among the elements of cultural which the family transmit to the child are his habits of eating, dressing and tradition of the family group (Burgess et al., 1963). Hence, the various practices are affected by family types. Family type had no bearing on the adoption of agricultural innovations (Kivlin et al., 1971). On the contrary, Jatlay (1977) reported that joint family system contributed for higher adoption of new agricultural practices. Joint families had higher level of health adoption (Kivlin et al., 1971). Hence, the adoption behaviour changes from one field to the other. Table 5.79 explains the influence of family type on practices of nutrition.

Table 5.79 : Differences in Practices of Nutrition Between Joint and Nuclear Families

Type of the Family	*N*	*M*	*SD*	*'t' value*
Joint	413	20.7046	5.3921	2.9363**
Nuclear	187	22.0695	5.2193	

** indicates significant at 0.01 level

It divulges from Table 5.79 that the obtained 't' value is highly significant and that the type of family has significant influence on practices of nutrition. This also indicates that respondents living in nuclear families are practicing more compared to joint families. In joint families it is difficult to bring in new practices because of various reasons. Hence, the null hypothesis, is rejected.

Family Size and Practices of Nutrition

Family size may sometimes provide a situation for learning good practices. On the other hand, the family size may be a hindrance for the adoption of new practices if it involves expenditure. The impact of family size in relation to nutrition practice is presented in Table 5.80.

Table 5.80 : Differences in Practices of Nutrition : Family Size-wise Analysis

Family Group	*N*	*M*	*SD*
Less than 4	173	21.7644	5.2868
5 – 6	193	21.6684	5.2179
7 – 8	125	20.576	5.4601
Above 8	108	19.7870	5.3904

The mean scores in the above Table reveal that the family size is associated with the practices and that higher the size of the family, lower is the practice score. To test whether these differences are significant, ANOVA technique has been employed. Table 5.81 gives the summary of analysis of variance.

Table 5.81 : Summary of ANOVA of Practice Scores of Instructors from Families of Vaired Sizes

Source of Variance	*df*	*Sum of squares*	*Mean of squares*	*'F'*
Between groups	3	359.125	119.7083	4.2011**
Within groups	596	16982.75	28.4946	
Total	**599**	**17341.875**		

** indicates significant at 0.01 level

The results indicate that the size of the family of the instructor is a significant factor which influences the practices of nutrition. (F is significant at 0.01 level of probability). Hence, the null hypothesis that 'there would not be significant influence of family size on the practices of nutrition', is rejected.

However, the analysis was further carried on to test the significant difference between the different sets of two groups by employing Kramer's multiple range test and the results are presented in Table 5.82.

The results in Table 5.82 indicate that the nutrition practices are more in the respondents with family size of less than four than the respondents whose family size is more than eight. This suggests that as the family size increases, the nutrition practices decreases, that means there is an inverse relationship between the size of the family and the practices of nutrition. The reasons are quite obvious.

Table 5.82 : Results of Kramer's Test Applied to Find the Significance of the Difference Among the Mean Practice Scores of Instructors of Different Family Sizes

	Above 8 members M_4	*7 – 8 members* M_3	*5 – 6 members* M_2	*Less than 4 members* M_1
N	108	125	193	174
M	19.7870	20.576	21.6684	21.7644

Note : 1. Any two means *not underscored* by the same line *are* significantly different.

2. Any two means *underscored* by the same line are *not* significantly different.

3. The means are arranged in ascending order from left to right

4. The level of significance employed in applying the Kramer's test is 0.05 level.

Experience and Practices of Nutrition

Experience is reported to be one of the significant factors which influence the practices of nutrition. 't' test was employed to know whether experience influences practices or not. The results of 't' test are given in Table 5.83.

It is clear from Table 5.83 that the calculated 't' value is

Table 5.83 : Experience-wise Differences in Practices of Nutrition

Group	*N*	*M*	*SD*	*'t' value*
Experience (more than one year)	306	21.7451	5.2025	2.8758**
Inexperienced (less than one year)	294	20.4898	5.4783	

** indicates significant at 0.01 level

significant beyond 0.01 level of probability. Hence, the null hypothesis, is rejected. If we observe the mean scores of the two groups, it is evident that the experienced instructors' mean score is higher than the inexperienced instructors' mean score. It can be concluded that the experience of the instructor has positive influence on the practices of nutrition.

Reading Newspapers and Practices of Nutrition

The basic function of the newspapers is to inform, analyse, appraise and criticize. The society obtains its information about current events from the newspaper and from other mass-media. By activating conversation and stimulating discussion, newspapers exert a constant influence on the opinions, values, attitudes and actions of the people (Mc Closky, 1967). The differences in practices of Readers and Non-Readers of newspapers are found in Table 5.84.

Table 5.84 : Readers and Non-Readers of Newspapers and Differences in Practices of Nutrition

Group	*N*	*M*	*SD*	*'t' value*
Readers	388	21.7680	5.1959	3.9180**
Non-Readers	212	19.9623	5.5029	

** indicates significant at 0.01 level

Data in Table 5.84 reveal that there exists significant difference in practices between readers and non-readers of newspapers as the obtained 't' value is significant. It indicates that readers of newspapers are practicing more compared to non-readers. Therefore, the null hypothesis, namely, 'there would not be significant influence of newspapers on nutrition practices', is rejected.

Listening to Radio and Practices of Nutrition

Since 78 per cent of India's population is in nearly 6,00,000 villages, rural radio broadcasting is of special significance. Further, the printed word can not go very far because of widespread illiteracy, the radio can be a significant medium of mass communication in rural areas. The radio can carry messages to the remote corner of the country and thus help to reduce rural isolation. In terms of reach and impact, a more powerful medium than the press to bring about changes in the practices of the people by providing knowledge base, is the radio. The differences in listeners and non-listeners of radio are brought out in Table 5.85.

Table 5.85 : Listeners and Non-Listeners of Radio and Differences in Practices of Nutrition

Group	*N*	*M*	*SD*	*'t' value*
Listeners	437	21.5515	5.2153	3.0614**
Non-listeners	163	20.0	5.6319	

** indicates significant at 0.01 level

A perusal of Table 5.85 makes it clear that the calculated 't' value between the mean scores of listeners and non-listeners of radio is significant at 0.01 level of probability for 598 degrees of freedom. This indicates that listening to radio and nutrition practices are significantly related. It also gives evidence that radio listening facilitated to practice more. Hence, the null hypothesis, is rejected.

Viewing Films and Practices of Nutrition

India now leads the world in the production of feature films. As a mass communication medium for bringing about the desired economic and social change in the country, the film can exert greater influence on the people than perhaps any other medium. Apart from its continued and growing popularity, the film is also far more effective medium of communication than other media, like newspapers and radio. Attending the films is highly related to agricultural adoption (Kivlin et al., 1971). The nutritional practice scores of viewers and non-viewers of films are noted in Table 5.86.

It is evident from Table 5.86 that there is an apparent difference between viewers and non-viewers of films, but that difference is not

Table 5.86 : Viewers and Non-Viewers of Films and Differences in Practices of Nutrition

Group	*N*	*M*	*SD*	*'t' value*
Viewers	526	21.1939	5.2994	0.7190^{NS}
Non-Viewers	74	20.6757	5.8728	

NS : indicates not significant

significant statistically as the calculated 't' value is below the tabulated value even at 0.05 level of probability. This means that there is no significant influence of films on nutrition practices. Hence, the null hypothesis that, 'there would not be significant influence of films on practices of nutrition', is retained.

Viewing of Filmshows and Practices of Nutrition

The filmshows screened in villages are meant to provide knowledge and to bring change in practices of the villagers. The good old practices in the field of health, nutrition or agriculture are to be modified for the betterment of the society and the individual. The changes may or may not involve expenditure. The influence of filmshows on the adoption behaviour is of great interest to nutrition educators and adult educators too. There is a presumption that those who are exposed to filmshows resort to good practices of nutrition than those who are not exposed. The differences in practices between viewers and non-viewers of filmshows are found in the Table 5.87.

Table 5.87 : Viewers and Non-viewers of Filmshows and Difference in Practices of Nutrition

Group	*N*	*M*	*SD*	*'t' value*
Viewers	203	22.0148	4.9175	3.0167**
Non-Viewers	397	20.6776	5.5419	

** indicates significant at 0.01 level

It is clear from the above table that there is a significant difference in the mean scores of nutrition practices between viewers and non-viewers of filmshows, as the obtained 't' value is significant. It means, viewing filmshows has a positive influence on nutritional practices and, hence, the null hypothesis is rejected. Though the filmshows have not shown any impact on knowledge and attitudes, it has impact on practices of nutrition among adult education instructors. It may be that the respondents by seeing filmshows might have acquired skills in cooking methods and selection of foodstuffs, etc.

Viewing of Television and Practices of Nutrition

Among all the available media of mass communication, Television is the most powerful. It combines the advantages of both visual and audio-media and is therefore more effective than Radio in providing awareness, information, application, trial and adoption (the five stages of adoption). In a vast country like India with widely differing (linguistically and culturally) segmented regions and people, Television can be a powerful instrument to bring about changes in the adoption behaviour. Thus, the messages of agriculture, nutrition, health and family planning can be popularized in more effective manner through Television than through any other medium. They bring about change in the adoption behaviour of the people (Pavalkar et al., 1978). Hence, Television can play a significant role in hastening the process of change in the individual (Rao, 1975). The differences in nutritional practices of viewers and non-viewers of Television are presented in the Table 5.88.

Table 5.88 : Viewers and Non-viewers of Television and Difference in Practices of Nutrition

Group	*N*	*M*	*SD*	*'t' value*
Viewers	185	22.0270	5.5082	2.6992**
Non-Viewers	415	20.7301	5.2673	

** indicates significant at 0.01 level

A perusal of the above Table reveals that the obtained 't' value is significant at 0.01 level of probability and, hence, viewing Television and practices are related. It also indicates that Television viewers' practices are more compared to non-viewers'.

Therefore, the null hypothesis that 'there would not be significant influence of Television on practices of nutrition', is rejected.

Summary of Results

In a nutshell, Table 5.89 gives all the results relating to the influence of different independent variables on dependent variables.

Table 5.89 : The Influence of Independent Variables on Dependent Variables and the Level of Significance

Sl. No.	*Socio, Economic and Demographic Variables*	*Knowledge*	*Attitudes*	*Practices*
1.	Age	0.05*	0.01**	NS***
2.	Sex	0.01	NS	0.01
3.	Annual Income of the Family	0.05	0.01	NS
4.	Caste	0.01	NS	0.05
5.	Religion	NS	NS	NS
6.	Marital Status	0.01	0.05	NS
7.	Occupation	0.01	0.05	NS
8.	Educational Status	0.01	0.01	0.01
9.	Family Type	0.01	0.05	0.01
10.	Size of the Family	0.01	0.05	0.01
11.	Experience as Adult Education Instructor	0.01	NS	0.01
12.	Reading Newspaper	0.05	NS	0.01
13.	Listening Radio	0.01	0.05	0.01
14.	Viewing Films	NS	NS	NS
15.	Viewing Filmshows	NS	NS	0.01
16.	Viewing of Television	NS	NS	0.01

* 0.05 indicates significance at 0.05 level

** 0.01 indicates significance at 0.01 level

*** NS indicates Note Significants

1. Age has significant influence on knowledge and attitude towards nutrition whereas it has not influenced significantly the practices of nutrition. Higher the age of the instructor the more the possession of knowledge and favourable attitudes toward nutrition. With regard to practices, there is no significant change in the practices of nutrition among instructors of different age-groups. Gupta (1981) and Sudha Rani (1987) also found that age

has significant influence on knowledge of nutrition. Sims (1976) and Kusuma (1987) found that mothers who are most knowledgeable about nutrition were younger and had less authoritarian attitudes about child rearing. Usha Devi (1983) found that age has no effect on nutritional knowledge. Thorndike (1968) concluded from his experiments that attitudes whether desirable or undesirable will be established as the age increases. As the age increases people resist to change. Their attitudes are not flexible as in their earlier years. Jalso et al., (1965) found a negative correlation between practices of nutrition and age of women. Sujatha (1978) and Kusuma (1987) reported the similar findings.

2. Sex has significant influence on knowledge and practices of nutrition whereas it could not influence attitudes toward nutrition. The female instructors were possessing significantly more knowledge than their counterparts. Sudha Rani (1987) reported similar findings. Contradicting the above results, Usha Devi (1983) found that both male and female organisers have equal amount of nutrition knowledge.

3. Annual income of the family has significant effect on the level of knowledge and attitudes toward nutrition. But it has no significant influence on practices. Higher economic status of the instructor facilitated to acquire more knowledge and to develop favourable attitude towards nutrition, whereas income has not shown any effect on the practices of nutrition among instructors. Sims (1976) and Gupta (1981) reported that higher the socio-economic status more is the knowledge in nutrition. In contrast, Kusuma (1987), Usha Devi (1983) and Sudha Rani (1987) found that income has no influence on knowledge of nutrition. Menon and Prema (1977), Muthayya (1974) and Kusuma (1987) found positive association between socio-economic status and attitudes toward nutrition. Arora et al., (1973), Datta Banik (1977), Venkatachalam et al., (1971). Sharma et al., (1977) and Kusuma (1987) reported that the income has no influence on practices of nutrition, whereas Jalso et al., (1965) found positive relationship between nutritional practices and socio-economic status.

4. Caste influenced significantly the knowledge and practices of nutrition, whereas it could not influence significantly the attitudes toward nutrition. Higher the caste in the social status better

was the knowledge and practice. The results were supported by Sudha Rani's (1987) study.

5. Religion has no significant influence on knowledge, attitudes and practices of nutrition. In contrast to the above findings, Arora et al., (1973) reported that different religious groups had different attitudes and practices of nutrition.

6. Marital status has significant influence on knowledge and attitudes toward nutrition, but it has no significant influence on practices of nutrition. Married instructors possessed more knowledge and favourable attitude towards nutrition than unmarried instructors. But there was no change in the practices between the two groups. Usha Devi (1983) and Sudha Rani (1987) reported that married people possessed more knowledge on nutrition than unmarried organisers.

7. Occupation of the instructor has significant influence on knowledge and attitudes toward nutrition, whereas it has not influenced the practices. Instructors other than those engaged in agricultural occupation had better knowledge and favourable attitudes toward nutrition whereas the nutritional practices were same in all occupational groups. Sims (1976) reported similar findings that nutrition knowledge and occupation are directly related. Muthaiah (1972) reported a direct and significant relationship between nutritional attitudes and occupation. Jalso et al., (1965) found that nutritional practices were directly related to occupation and these results contradict the findings of the present study.

8. Educational status of the instructor has significant influence on knowledge, attitudes and practices of nutrition. Higher the education better was the knowledge, attitudes and practices among instructors. Alford and Tibbets (1971) and Jalso et al., (1965) found that nutritional practices were directly related to education.

9. Family type has significant influence on knowledge, attitudes and practices of nutrition among adult education instructors. Instructors belonging to nuclear families had high knowledge, favourable attitudes and better practices of nutrition than instructors from joint families. Gupta (1981) reported that no

significant difference existed in the nuclear and joint family adolescents on the nutritional knowledge.

10. Family size of the instructor had significant influence on knowledge, attitudes and practices of nutrition. Family size of the instructor was negatively related to nutritional knowledge, attitudes and practices. Instructors belonging to small families had better nutritional knowledge, favourable attitudes and better practices than instructors of larger families. Sims (1976) reported the similar findings.

11. Experience as an adult education instructor significantly influenced the knowledge and practices, whereas it has no influence on the attitude towards nutrition.

12. There was significant influence of Newspaper on knowledge and practices of nutrition. But it did not significantly influence the attitudes toward nutrition.

13. Listening to Radio had significant influence on knowledge, attitudes and practices of nutrition among adult education instructors.

14. Viewing Films (feature) had no significant effect on knowledge, attitudes and practices of nutrition among adult education instructors.

15. Viewing Filmshows had significant impact only on the practices of nutrition, whereas it was not so on knowledge and on attitudes toward nutrition.

16. Viewing Television has significant influence on the practices of nutrition, but it could not influence the knowledge and attitude towards nutrition.

Out of 16 socio, economic and demographic variables, 12 variables (Age, Sex, Annual Income of the Family, Caste, Marital Status, Occupation, Educational Status, Family Type, Size of the Family, Experience as an Adult Education Instructor, Reading Newspaper and Listening to Radio) have significant influence on knowledge, whereas four variables (Religion, Viewing Films, Viewing Filmshows and Viewing Television) have no significant influence on knowledge.

The influence of eight variables (Age, Annual Income of the Family, Marital Status, Occupation, Educational Status, Family Type, Size of the Family and Listening to Radio) on attitudes is evident, whereas there is no such influence on attitudes by other eight variables (Sex, Caste, Religion, Experience as an Adult Education Instructor, Reading Newspaper, Viewing Films, Viewing Filmshows and Viewing Television).

Ten variables (Sex, Caste, Educational Status, Family Type, Size of the Family, Experience as an Adult Education Instructor, Reading Newspaper, Listening to Radio, Viewing Filmshows and Viewing Television) have influence on nutritional practices and six variables (Age, Annual Income of the Family, Religion, Marital Status, Occupation and Viewing Films) have no influence on nutritional practices.

Section – 3

Correlation Analysis

Inter-relationship Among Knowledge, Attitude and Practice

In this part, correlation coefficients were presented to know the inter-relationship among knowledge, attitude and practices. Results of multiple regression analysis were also presented to indicate the contribution of independent variables for predicting the variance in knowledge, attitudes and practices of nutrition. The relationship between knowledge, attitudes and practices are shown in Table 5.90.

Table 5.90 : Correlation Between the Variables

Variables	*Simple Correlation Values*	*Partial Correlation Values*	*Level of Significance*
Knowledge & Attitudes	0.5668	0.3897	1% level
Knowledge & Practices	0.6139	0.4706	1% level
Attitude & Practice	0.4851	0.2109	1% level

From the above Table, it is clear that 'r' values (simple correlation) 0.5668 between knowledge and attitude, 0.6139 between knowledge and practice and 0.4851 between attitude and practice are significant at 0.01 level. It means that there is a close association between the three variables. It is also evident that the correlation ('r' value) between knowledge and practice is greater than other two 'r' values, which denotes that influence of knowledge over practice is greater than the influence of knowledge over practice is greater than the influence of attitudes over practices. It is proved that knowledge, attitudes and practices are positively inter-related, and, hence, the hypothesis 'that there exists significant and positive inter-relationship among the three dependent variables', is accepted.

Even by looking at the partial correlation values in the above Table, it is understood that the relationship between knowledge and practice is more than double to that of attitudes and practices when the effect of attitudes is statistically controlled or partialled out. Although all the three partial 'r' values are notably lower than simple correlations, they are statistically significant at 0.01 level of probability. The data establishes the inter-dependency of these three variables and the cause and effect relationship among these variables is described below to obtain a theoretical conceptualization with the help of already established models of relationship.

In the present study instructors who have good knowledge in nutrition showed better nutritional practices. As the knowledge of nutrition in adult education instructors increases their nutritional practices also increased.

This finding was supported by the studies of Bell and Lamb (1973), Lovett et al., (1970), Carruth et al., (1971) and Alford and Tibbets (1971).

Contrary to the above results, Amudson (1956), Krause and Fox (1977) showed that nutritional knowledge did not influence the nutritional practices.

Peterson and Kies (1972), Schwartz (1975), Carruth (1977) found in their studies that attitudes influence nutritional practices, independent of the individual's knowledge of nutritional concepts. Lewin (1943), Baker (1972) and Hays and Emmons (1973) reported that some nutritional practices are subject to modification without gain in knowledge and a positive change in attitude.

In contrast Weigel (1976) reported that attitudes could not influence the practices unless it is assisted with adequate knowledge in the context of health education.

It is also quite evident from the present study that instructors who have goôd knowledge in nutrition showed favourable attitudes toward nutritional practices than the instructors who have poor knowledge in nutrition. This fact was supported by the study of Schwartz (1975) who investigated the nature of relationship of nutritional knowledge to attitudes and the inter-relationship of knowledge and attitudes with practices among the subjects. He found the relationship of knowledge/ attitudes and attitude/practices (K⟷A⟷P). It was found that knowledge is very much essential for developing desirable attitudes and this in turn influence nutritional practices.

Among the four models adopted by Schwartz (1975) using three variables, Knowledge—Attitude—Practice (K—A—P), the K—A—P model IV is suited to the present study. The relationship between the knowledge, attitudes and practices in this study can be pictured in this way.

K — A — P model IV

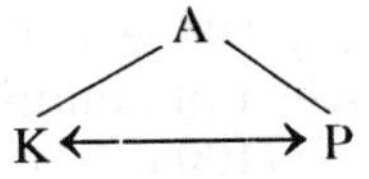

```
      A
     / \
K <------> P
```

Knowledge influence practices both directly and indirectly as mediated by attitudes concurrently. The findings of Sujatha (1978) also support this model.

Prediction of Knowledge, Attitudes and Practice of Nutrition

The knowledge, attitudes and practices are the most complex phenomena. As already seen in the previous section of this chapter many variables or factors influence the level of knowledge, attitudes and practices of instructors. The complexity of these three variables includes not only the influence of innumerable variables on them, but also the varied amount of influence by each of the independent variables. Again, the complex nature of knowledge, attitudes and practices include many variations between individuals, situations and times. So, it may be very difficult to find out all the variables which explain the major part of the variance in knowledge, attitude and practice.

In the following pages, the contribution of 16 independent socio, economic and demographic variables put together and of each variable in predicting the knowledge, attitude and practices in nutrition are presented and discussed along with the relevant prediction equations.

Prediction of Knowledge (K) of Nutrition with Socio, Economic and Demographic Variables

Multiple (step-wise) regression analysis, was carried out with the help of 16 independent variables to derive an equation, to predict knowledge and to identify the amount of contribution made by each variable in explaining the variance in knowledge. The summary of each step of the multiple regression analysis (which is the output of computer analysis) is given in Table 5.91.

From Table 5.91 it is evident that the first variable that entered into the multiple (step-wise) regression analysis in sex (S). The multiple correlation 'R' is 0.1555 which is nothing but the simple correlation shown in column 11 between knowledge and the sex. The relationship is negative, i.e., the female instructors have more knowledge than male. It can also be observed from the Table that 'R' is significant at 0.01 level (F = 14.828 for 1, 598 degrees of freedom). The coefficient of multiple determination (R^2) disclosed that about 2.42 per cent (100 R^2) of the variance in knowledge is accounted for by sex alone in the first step. The standard error of multiple estimate (SE of 'R') 6.9341 shown in column 5 revealed that nearly 68 per cent of the obtained knowledge scores will lie within the range of ± 6.9341 points of predicted knowledge scores.

The partial regression coefficient (b) presented in column 7 is –2.1904. The 't' values for 'b' (column 8) is significant at 0.01 level. The constant value that will be considered in the equation, at the end of the first step, with which the prediction of knowledge can be made is shown in column 9. The general form of the prediction equation may be given as

$$X' = A + b_1x_1 + b_2x_2 + b_3x_3 + \dots\dots\dots\dots + b_nx_n.$$

where X' denotes the predicted score of dependent variable

'A' is the constant

b_1, b_2, b_3 .... b_n are partial regression coefficients and x_1, x_2, x_3, ... x_n are the obtained values on different independent variables

Thus the actual equation at the end of the first step will be

$$K = 37.1498 — 2.1904\ S \qquad (1.1)$$

Table 5.91 : Multiple (Step-wise) Regression Analysis—Dependent Variable : Knowledge (K) : Independent Variables : Socio, Economic and Demographic Factors

Step No.	Independent variable entered in each step	Multiple correlation 'R'	R^2	Standard error of multiple correlation	'F' value (d.f) and level of significance	'b' coefficient (or) partial regression coefficient	't' value for 'b' and level of significance	Constant	'β' Coefficient	Simple coefficient of correlation with dependent variable and its level of significance	% of variance in the dependent variable explained by each variable
(1)	(2)	(3)	(4)	(5)	(6)	(7)	(8)	(9)	(10)	(11)	(12)
1.	Sex	0.1555	0.02419	6.9341	14.8281 ** (1,598)	–2.1904	3.8507**	37.1498	–0.1556	–0.156**	2.42
2.	Education	0.2381	0.05671	6.8233	17.9457 ** (2,597)	–2.6363 1.335	4.6389** 4.5362**	35.2200	–0.1872 0.1831	0.151**	2.91
3.	Age	0.2937	0.08631	6.7210	18.7687 ** (3,596)	–3.2024 1.2057 1.0757	5.5750** 4.8878** 4.3947**	33.1579	–0.2274 0.1947 0.1766	0.122**	3.53 2.93 2.16
4.	Radio listening	0.3215	0.10341	6.6634	17.1577 ** (4,595)	–3.5114 1.1581 1.0650 2.0297	6.0873** 4.7277** 4.3883** 3.3685**	30.2657	–0.2494 0.1871 0.1749 0.1331	0.183**	3.87 2.81 2.13 1.50
5.	Size of the family	0.3369	0.11348	6.6315	15.2076 ** (5,594)	–3.2704 1.1221 1.0187 1.9773 –0.6676	5.6238** 4.5953** 4.2065** 3.2955** 2.5969**	31.7067	–0.2322 0.1812 0.1673 0.1297 –0.1018	–0.147**	3.61 2.73 2.04 1.47 1.49
6.	Experience as an Adult Education Instructor	0.3523	0.12414	6.5971	14.0079 ** (6,593)	–3.0571 1.1497 0.8700 1.8224 –0.7244 1.4716	5.2354** 4.7287** 3.5195** 3.0392** 2.8229** 2.6859**	29.8658	–0.2171 0.1857 0.1429 0.1195 –0.1104 0.1070	0.142**	3.38 2.79 1.75 1.35 1.62 1.52

Note : * indicates significant at 0.05 level ** indicates significant at 0.01 level NS–indicates not significant

As the partial regression coefficients were not significant from the step 7, the further details were not given.

Education (ED) entered into the step-wise regression analysis as the second most significant variable. The multiple correlation obtained between knowledge on one side and the two independent variables, viz., sex and education on the other side is 0.238. Thus the strength of the relationship between knowledge and the two independent variables put together is about 23.8 per cent. The relationship is significant at 0.01 level as the F value, 17.9457 is far beyond the Table value for 2 and 597 degrees of freedom. The two variables put together can explain about 5.67 per cent (R^2 = 0.0567) of the variance in knowledge. Out of this, 2.91 per cent of the variance is explained by sex and the remaining 2.75 per cent is accounted for by education (column 12 of the Table). It is evident that by including education, the contribution of sex is enhanced from 2.42 per cent to 2.91 per cent and this may be due to inter-correlation between the two predictor variables (column 12). These percentages are obtained by multiplying the Beta coefficients (—Standard Partial Coefficients) with the corresponding simple correlations between the dependent variables and the respective independent variable (column 10 and 11 × 100).

The Standard Error of multiple estimate (SE of R) in column 5 revealed that nearly 68 per cent of the obtained knowledge scores will lie within the range of ±6.8233 points of predicted scores of knowledge of nutrition. The partial regression coefficients shown in column 7 disclosed, when education is included as predictor variables, that the knowledge will increase by 1.1335 points for every unit increase in education. Both the partial regression coefficients are significant at 0.01 level as shown in column 8. The regression equation to predict knowledge with sex and education as predictor variables is

$$K = 35.2200 — 2.6363\ S + 1.1335\ ED \qquad (1.2)$$

where 35.2200 is the constant to be considered at this step and –2.6363 and 1.1335 are the partial regression coefficients.

In the hierarchy of predictor variables associated with knowledge, age (A) entered as the next important variable. The multiple correlation or the combined association of S, ED and A with knowledge is 0.294 which is significant at 0.01 level (F = 18.7687 for 3 and 596 degrees of freedom). The value of R^2 (0.0863) disclosed that about 8.6 per cent of variance in knowledge is explained by these three variables. Out of this variance 3.53 per cent, 2.93 per cent and 2.16 per cent are explained by S, ED and A respectively. It is observed that by including age as one more predictor variable, the variance accounted for by S and ED has gone up from 2.91 per cent to 3.53 per cent and 2.75 per cent to 2.93 per cent due to inter-correlations prevailed among the three independent variables. The Standard Error of multiple estimate indicate that as many as 68 per cent of the obtained knowledge scores will lie within the range of ±6.7210 points of predicted scores of knowledge. When these three predictor variables are considered, the partial regression coefficients indicate that the increase in knowledge is by –3.2024, 1.2057 and 1.0757 unit for every unit increase in S, ED and A respectively. All the three partial regression coefficients are significant at 0.01 level as shown in column 8. The regression equation at this step with the constant of 33.1579 will be

$$K = 33.1579 — 3.2024\ S + 1.2057\ ED + 1.0757\ A \qquad (1.3)$$

The next variable entered the step-wise regression analysis is Listening to Radio (LR). The multiple — R is 0.322 and this is significant beyond 0.01 level. It revealed that the combined strength of relationship between knowledge the related variables, viz., S, ED, A and LR is 32 per cent. Thus the increase in the 'R' is 2.0 per cent only.

All the four predictor variables put together can explain 10.34 per cent ($R^2 = 0.1034$) of the variance in knowledge of nutrition. The variance explained by the variables Sex, Education, Age and Listening to Radio are 3.87 per cent, 2.81 per cent, 2.13 per cent and 1.50 per cent respectively. The equation at this step will be as follows

$$K = 30.2657 — 3.5114\ S + 1.1581\ ED + 1.0650\ A + 2.0297\ LR \qquad (1.4)$$

The next variable that entered into the analysis is Size of the Family (SF). The multiple 'R' is significant and the strength of the relationship is 33.69 per cent between knowledge and host of five predictor variables. All the five variables, viz., S, ED, A, LR and SF put together can explain 11.35 per cent of the variance in knowledge. The percentage of variance explained by the variables, namely, Sex, Education, Age, Listening to Radio and Size of the Family are 3.61, 2.73, 2.04, 1.47 and 1.49 respectively. The individual variable's contributions are obtained by multiplying the Beta Coefficients (column 10) with the corresponding simple correlations (column 11) between the predictor variables and knowledge of nutrition and they are shown in column 12. The partial regression coefficients are significant at 0.01 level. The regression equation can be written with five predictor variables as

$$K = 31.7067 - 3.2704\ S + 1.1221\ ED + 1.0187\ A + 1.9773\ LR - 0.6676\ SF \qquad (1.5)$$

The variable that entered into the sixth step is Experience (Ex) as an adult education instructor. All the six variables put together can explain 12.41 per cent of variance in the knowledge of nutrition ($R^2 = 0.12414$) and the combined strength of relationship between the knowledge and the six predictor variables is 35.23 per cent ($R = 0.3523$). The partial regression coefficients are significant at 0.01 level. The equation with six predictor variables will be

$$K = 29.8658 - 3.0571\ S + 1.1497\ ED + 0.8700\ A + 1.8224\ LR - 0.7244\ SF + 1.4716\ Ex \qquad (1.6)$$

As it is evident from Table 5.91 the six factors, namely, Sex, Education, Age, Listening to Radio, Size of the Family and Experience as an instructor have turned out to be the significant predictors of knowledge of nutrition. The 't' values of the partial regression coefficients of these six factors are significant beyond the 0.05 level of probability. The remaining ten variables do not contribute to the knowledge significantly as their partial regression coefficients are not significant. All the 16 factors put together can explain only 14.36 per cent of variance in knowledge as revealed by computer analysis. The six significant factors put together can explain as much as 12.41 per cent of variance in knowledge of nutrition and the percentage of variance explained by six variables individually are : Sex 3.38, Education 2.79, Age 1.75, Listening to Radio 1.35, Size of the Family 1.62 and Experience as an adult education instructor 1.52. The unexplained variance in knowledge may be due to the factors not covered in this study.

The data presented above would indicate that out of 16 socio, economic and demographic variables, only six variables contribute significantly to the prediction of 'knowledge on nutrition' and they include Sex, Education, Age, Listening to Radio, Size of the Family and Experience as an adult education instructor. The total variance explained by the six variables put together would come to 12.41 per cent, the percentage of variance explained by them individually being 3.38, 2.79, 1.75, 1.35, 1.62 and 1.52 respectively. It means that the extent or amount of contribution of these variables to the prediction of knowledge on nutrition is different. Therefore, the hypothesis that 'the contribution of socio, economic and demographic variables in predicting the knowledge of nutrition among adult education instructors would not vary significantly', is rejected.

Prediction of Attitudes (A) with Socio, Economic and Demographic Variables

The contribution of each of the 16 predictor variables in predicting attitudes toward nutrition is presented in Table 5.92 and discussed.

It divulges from Table 5.92 that Education (ED) stood as the first variable having very strong association with Attitudes. The multiple correlation obtained, i.e., 0.1898 is significant at 0.01 level (F = 22.3507 for 1 and 598 degrees of freedom). Education explains 3.60 per cent of variance in attitudes as R^2 is 0.03602. The partial regression coefficient, 2.5716 indicates that Attitudes increased by 2.5716 units for every unit increase in Education. The 'b' coefficient is significant at 0.01 level (t = 4.7277). The regression equation with education as predictor variable will be

$$A = 11.6336 + 2.5716 \text{ ED} \qquad (2.1)$$

In the second step the additional predictor variable that entered into the regression analysis is Size of the Family (FS). Next to Education, Family Size commanded stronger relationship with Attitudes among the remaining variables. The multiple 'R' is 0.2212 which revealed that the strength of relationship between the dependent variables and the two independent variables, viz., Education and Family Size is about 22 per cent. The 'F' value obtained in the test for significance of multiple 'R' is 15.3698 for 2 and 597 degrees of freedom and it is significant beyond 0.01 level. The two variables put together can explain 4.89 per cent of variance in attitude towards nutrition (100 R^2) and out of 4.89 per cent of the variance explained by the two predictor variables, the contribution of Education is 3.54 per cent and that of Family Size is 1.35 per cent. These individual contributions of variables are obtained by calculating the products of Beta coefficients and the corresponding simple correlation coefficients which are shown in column 10 and 11 in the Table 5.92 and

Table 5.92 : Multiple (Step-wise) Regression Analysis—Dependent Variable : Attitude (A) : Independent Variables : Socio, Economic and Demographic Factors

Step No.	Independent variable entered in each step	Multiple correlation 'R'	R^2	Standard error of multiple correlation	'F' value (d.f) and level of significance	'b' coefficient (or) partial regression coefficient	't' value for 'b' and level of significance	Constant	'β' Coefficient	Simple coefficient of correlation with dependent variable and its level of significance	% of variance in the dependent variable explained by each variable
(1)	(2)	(3)	(4)	(5)	(6)	(7)	(8)	(9)	(10)	(11)	(12)
1.	Education	0.1898	0.03602	15.0813	22.3507 ** (1,598)	2.5716	4.7277**	112.6336	0.1898	0.1980**	3.60
2.	Size of the family	0.2212	0.04896	14.9922	15.3698 ** (2,597)	2.5269	4.6710**	116.4595	0.1865	–0.119**	3.54
						–1.6338	2.8500**		–0.1138		1.35
3.	Age	0.2464	0.06071	14.9118	12.8422 ** (3,596)	2.5678	4.7703**	112.4998	0.1895	0.108**	3.59
						–1.5728	2.7562**		–0.1095		1.31
						1.4461	2.7303**		0.1085		1.17
4.	Occupation	0.2639	0.06968	14.8529	11.1424 ** (4,595)	2.6490	4.9309**	108.2052	0.1955	0.060^{NS}	3.71
						–1.4700	2.5789*		–0.1024		1.22
						1.7923	3.2766**	0.1345		1.45	
						1.2577	2.3951*		0.0985		0.59
5.	Annual Income of the Family	0.2756	0.07600	14.8149	9.7719 ** (5,594)	2.6311	4.9096**	104.9037	0.1942	0.089*	3.69
						–1.3823	2.4241*		–0.0963		1.15
						1.7837	3.2692**		0.1338		1.44
						1.3123	2.5022*		0.1028		0.61
						1.1872	2.0151		0.0798		0.71

Note : * indicates significant at 0.05 level ** indicates significant at 0.01 level NS–indicates not significant

As the partial regression coefficients were not significant from the step 6, the further details were not given.

multiplying with 100 (100 R^2). The partial regression coefficients of the two predictor variables are significant at 0.01 level (column 8). With the constant value 116.4595, obtained at this step, the equation will be

$$A = 116.4595 + 2.5269\ ED - 1.6338\ FS \tag{2.2}$$

Age (Ag) entered as the next important variable into the regression analysis in step number 3. The combined or cumulated strength of relationship between these three predictor variables and attitudes is 24.6 per cent (R = 0.2462). The multiple 'R' is significant at 0.01 (F = 12.8422 for 3 and 596 degrees of freedom). The value of coefficient of multiple determination R^2 is 0.06071 Therefore, the three variables together can explain 6.07 per cent of variance in the attitude. Out of this, the three predictor variables individually contributed 3.59 per cent, 1.30 per cent and 1.16 per cent of the variance in the dependent variable (see column 12 of the Table).

The partial regression coefficients at this step reveals that for every unit increase in Education, Family Size and Age, the attitudes of nutrition will increase by 2.5678, –1.5728 and 1.4461 units respectively. All the three coefficients are found to be significant at 0.01 level. The regression equation to predict attitudes with three variables can be written as

$$A = 112.4998 + 2.5678\ ED - 1.5728\ FS + 1.4461\ Ag \tag{2.3}$$

The fourth predictor variable that entered into the analysis is occupation (OC). The combined strength of relationship between the four variables — ED, FS, Ag and OC and attitudes is 26.4 per cent (R = 0.264). The variance explained by all the four predictor variables is 6.97 per cent (R^2 = 0.0697) and out of this, the contribution made by each variable is : Education 3.71 per cent, Size of the Family 1.22 per cent, Age 1.45 per cent and Occupation 0.59 per cent. The equation at this step will be as follows

$$A=108.2052+2.6490\ ED-1.4700\ FS+1.7923\ Ag+1.2577\ OC \tag{2.4}$$

Annual Income (AI) is the next most significant predictor variable in the analysis. The multiple 'R' which is significant at 0.01 level is found to be 0.276. The total variance explained in the dependent variable by the host of five variables is 7.60 per cent. The percentage of variance individually explained by the variables Education, Size of the Family, Age, Occupation and Annual Income is 3.69, 1.15, 1.44, 0.61 and 0.71 respectively. The partial regression coefficients are significant either at 0.01 level or at 0.05 level. The regression equation can be written with five predictor variables as

$$A = 104.9037 + 2.6311\ ED - 1.3823\ FS + 1.7837\ Ag + 1.3123\ OC + 1.1872\ AI \qquad (2.5)$$

The summary of the Table reveals that the five factors, namely, Education Size of the Family, Age, Occupation and Annual Income have been turned out to be significant factors. The percentage of variance explained by the sixteen factors put together is 9.6 per cent of variance in attitudes whereas the first five factors put together can explain as much as 7.5 per cent of variance in attitudes of instructors. The remaining factors have not been shown in the Table because their partial regression coefficients are not significant. Hence, it can be concluded that the equation No. 2.5 will be best equation to predict attitudes of instructors toward nutrition.

A glance through the data presented above would indicate that out of 16 socio, economic and demographic variables, only five variables contribute significantly to the prediction of 'Attitudes toward Nutrition' and they are Education, Size of the Family, Age, Occupation and Annual Income. The total variance explained by the five variables put together would come to 7.6 per cent, the percentage of variance explained by them individually being 3.69, 1.15, 1.44, 0.61 and 0.71 respectively. It means that the extent or amount of contribution of these variables to the prediction of attitudes toward nutrition is different. Therefore, the hypothesis that 'there would not be any significant variation in the amount of contribution made by different socio, economic and demographic variables to the prediction of attitudes of adult education instructors toward nutrition', is rejected.

Prediction of Practices (P) with Socio, Economic and Demographic Factors

In this part, practices (P) of nutrition was predicted with the help of socio, economic and demographic variables as predictor variables. As above, the step-wise regression analysis was carried out and the summary of the computer output is given in Table 5.93 for each step.

Table 5.93 : Multiple (Step-wise) Regression Analysis—Dependent Variable : Practice (P) : Independent Variables : Socio, Economic and Demographic Factors

Step No.	Independent variable entered in each step	Multiple correlation 'R'	R^2	Standard error of multiple correlation	'F' value (d.f) and level of significance	'b' coefficient (or) partial regression coefficient	't' value for 'b' and level of significance	Constant	'β' Coefficient	Simple coefficient of correlation with dependent variable and its level of significance	% of variance in the dependent variable explained by each variable
(1)	(2)	(3)	(4)	(5)	(6)	(7)	(8)	(9)	(10)	(11)	(12)
1.	Education	0.1691	0.02862	5.3075	17.6194 ** (1,598)	0.8035	4.1975**	19.2725	0.1692	0.169**	2.86
2.	Sex	0.2246	0.05047	5.2518	15.8682 ** (2,597)	0.9269 –1.6215	4.8192** 3.7069**	21.4980	0.1951 –0.1501	–0.116**	3.30 1.74
3.	Reading Newspaper on Nutrition matters	0.2841	0.08074	5.1718	17.4479 ** (3,596)	0.8380 –1.9868 1.9727	4.4001** 4.5301** 4.4298**	19.0140	0.1764 –0.1839 0.1788	0.165**	2.98 2.14 2.95
4.	Type of the family	0.3130	0.09797	5.1274	16.1576 ** (4,595)	0.8025 –1.9362 2.1691 –1.2074	4.2435** 4.4503** 4.8707** 3.3719**	20.7586	0.1690 –0.1792 0.1966 –0.1327	–0.121**	2.85 2.08 3.24 1.61
5.	Experience as an Adult Education Instructor	0.3302	0.10904	5.10014	14.5401 ** (5,594)	0.8334 –1.8401 2.0674 –1.2916 1.1234	4.4224** 4.2379** 4.6505** 3.6123** 2.7161**	19.1499	0.1755 –0.1703 0.1874 –0.1420 0.1065	0.107**	2.96 1.98 3.09 1.72 1.14
6.	Size of the family	0.3424	0.11724	5.0809	13.1272 ** (6,593)	0.8138 –1.7122 2.1004 –1.0149 1.1504 –0.4874	4.3304** 3.9272** 4.7404** 2.7052** 2.7909** 2.3474*	19.5393	0.1713 –0.1585 0.1904 –0.1116 0.1091 –0.0968	–0.136**	2.89 1.84 3.14 1.35 1.17 1.32

Note : * indicates significant at 0.05 level ** indicates significant at 0.01 level NS–indicates not significant

As the partial regression coefficients were not significant from the step 7, the further details were not given.

In the first step of the analysis, Education (ED) entered as the most prominent variable. The multiple 'R' 0.169 is significant at 0.01 level (F = 17.6194 for 1 and 598 degrees of freedom). The coefficient of multiple determination is 0.0286. That means only about 2.86 per cent of the variance in the dependent variable (P) can be explained by Education (ED). The equation at the first step will be

$$P = 19.2725 + 0.8035\ ED \qquad (3.1)$$

Sex (S) is the next variable that entered into the analysis. The multiple 'R', 0.225 is significant at 0.01 level. The total variance that can be explained in the dependent variable, P, by the two independent variables, Education and Sex is 5.05 per cent, out of which the contribution of ED is 3.30 per cent and the remaining 1.75 per cent is accounted for by Sex. The partial regression coefficients for ED and S are significant at 0.01 level. The constant that should be taken into account is 21.4980 and the prediction equation at the end of this step will be

$$P = 21.4980 + 0.9269\ ED - 1.6215\ S \qquad (3.2)$$

Newspaper Reading (NR) is the next variable that entered into the analysis. The multiple 'R' increased from 0.225 to 0.284. Thus all the three predictor variables put together can explain only 8.07 per cent of variance in the practice, whereas the variance explained by three variables individually are : Education 2.98 per cent, Sex 2.14 per cent and Newspaper Reading 2.95 per cent. The partial regression coefficients for all the three variables, i.e., ED, S and NR are highly significant. The prediction equation can be written as

$$P = 19.0140 + 0.8380\ ED - 1.9868\ S + 1.9727\ NR \qquad (3.3)$$

The fourth predictor that entered into the analysis is Type of the Family (TF). The combined strength of relationship between the four variables — ED, S, NR and TF and practice is 31.3 per cent (R = 0.313). The variance that can be explained by all the four predictor variables is 9.79 per cent (R^2 = 0.979). The percentage of variance explained by the variables, namely, Education, Sex, Newspaper Reading and Type of the Family are 2.85, 2.08, 3.24 and 1.61 respectively. The contribution of each variable, the standard error of multiple estimate, the level of significance and the partial regression coefficients of all the variables are significant at 0.01 level. The equation at this step will be as follows :

$$P = 20.7586 + 0.8025\ ED - 1.9362\ S + 2.1691\ NR - 1.2075\ TF \quad (3.4)$$

Experience (Ex) is the next significant predictor variable in the analysis. The multiple 'R' which is significant at 0.01 level, is found to be 0.330. The total variance that can be explained in nutrition practices by the host of five variables is 10.9 per cent. The variance explained by the variables Education, Sex, Newspaper Reading, Type of the Family and Experience as an adult education instructor are 2.96 per cent, 1.98 per cent, 3.09 per cent, 1.72 per cent and 1.14 per cent respectively. All the partial regression coefficients are found to be significant at 0.01 level. The equation at this step of the analysis can be written as

$$P = 19.1499 + 0.8334\ ED - 1.8401\ S + 2.0674\ NR - 1.2916\ TF + 1.1234\ Ex \quad (3.5)$$

The variable entered into the sixth step is the Size of the Family (SF). All the six variables put together can explain 11.72 per cent of variance in the practice of nutrition ($R^2 = 0.1172$) and the combined strength of six predictor variables is 34.24 per cent ($R = 0.3424$). The variance explained by six variables individually are : Education 2.89 per cent, Sex 1.84 per cent, Newspaper Reading 3.14 per cent, Type of the Family 1.35 per cent, Experience as an adult education instructor 1.17 per cent and Size of the Family 1.32 per cent. The prediction equation at this step with the constant value and the partial regression coefficients shown in columns 9 and 7 respectively will be

$$P = 19.5393 + 0.8138\ ED - 1.7122\ S + 2.1004\ NR - 1.0149\ TF + 1.1504\ Ex - 0.4874\ SF \quad (3.6)$$

The obtained 't' values (Table 5.93) of the partial regression coefficients of the factors, viz., Education, Sex, Newspaper, Type of the Family, Experience and Size of the Family are significant. This indicates that these factors have turned out to be the significant predictors of the practices of nutrition. All the sixteen factors put together can explain only 13.24 per cent of variance in practices whereas the first six factors put together can explain as much as 11.72 per cent of variance. Hence, it can be concluded that these six factors are the only significant predictors of practices of nutrition among adult education instructors.

It is evident from the above data that out of 16 socio, economic and demographic variables, only six contribute significantly to the prediction of 'practices of nutrition' and they are Education, Sex, Newspaper Reading, Type of the Family, Experience as an adult education instructor and Size of the Family. The total variance explained by the six variables put together would come to 11.72 per cent, the percentage of variance explained by them individually being 2.89, 1.84, 3.14, 1.35, 1.17 and 1.32 respectively. It means that the extent or amount of contribution of these variables to the prediction of practices of nutrition is different. Hence, the hypothesis that, 'the contribution of socio, economic and demographic variables in predicting the practices of nutrition among adult education instructors would not vary significantly', is rejected.

Summary of Results

For a quick survey, the variables that contribute significantly for predicting knowledge, attitudes and practices along with percentage of variable explained are noted in Table 5.94.

Age, Sex, Educational Status, Size of the Family, Experience as an Adult Education Instructor and Listening to Radio are the significant variables that contribute to the prediction of knowledge and their contributions are different.

Age, Annual Income of the Family, Occupation, Educational Status and Size of the Family Variables significantly contribute to the prediction of attitudes and they have differential contribution.

The variables that contribute significantly to the prediction of practices are Sex, Educational Status, Family Type, Size of the Family, Experience as an Adult Education Instructor and Reading Newspaper. The contribution made by them are not same.

It can also be observed that the percentage of variance explained in knowledge, attitudes and practices by each independent variable is different.

Comparison of Results of Section–2 with Section–3

The results of Section–2, i.e., "Influence of Independent Variables on Dependent Variables" merely indicate the presence or absence of influence of each of the 16 socio, economic and demographic variables independently on knowledge, attitudes and practices and they do not show the exact quantity of influence of one

Table 5.94 : Significant Socio, Economic and Demographic Variables for Predicting Knowledge, Attitudes and Practices Along with the Percentage of Variance Explained

Sl. No.	*Socio, Economic and Demographic Variables*	*Knowledge*	*Attitudes*	*Practices*
1.	Age	1.75	1.44	--
2.	Sex	3.38	--	1.84
3.	Annual Income of the Family	--	0.71	--
4.	Caste			
5.	Religion			
6.	Marital Status			
7.	Occupation	--	0.61	--
8.	Educational Status	2.79	3.69	2.89
9.	Family Type	--	--	1.35
10.	Size of the Family	1.62	1.15	1.32
11.	Experience as Adult Education Instructor	1.52	--	1.17
12.	Reading Newspaper	--	--	3.14
13.	Listening Radio	1.35	--	--
14.	Viewing Films			
15.	Viewing Filmshows			
16.	Viewing of Television			

variable on the other. The results got in Section – 3 "Correlational Analysis" by employing the step-wise regression analysis technique indicate not only, whether the variable has influence or not but also the extent of influence of the variable when it is jointly acting with other variables. The variables that appeared to have influence on knowledge, attitudes and practices independently may loose their influence when they are combined with other variables because of inter-relationships among them.

By comparing the results in Tables 5.89 and 5.94, it can be further inferred that (1) the variables, viz., Annual Income of the Family, Caste, Marital Status, Occupation, Family Type and Reading

Newspaper which have influence individually on knowledge did not significantly contribute to the prediction of knowledge and did not enter into the prediction equation. This may be due to the inter-relationship of these variables with the six significant variables that emerged from the step-wise regression analysis.

In the case of attitudes, the variables namely Marital Status, Family Type and Listening to Radio which have influenced independently did not have such influence when combined with the 16 variables. Perhaps this may be due to inter-correlations between these variables and the five significant variables that come out from step-wise regression analysis.

Variables, namely, Caste, Listening to Radio, Viewing Filmshows and Viewing Television which influenced nutritional practices independently have lost their influence in the presence of the sixteen variables and probably this may be due to the fact that there exist inter-relationships between these variables and six significant predictors of nutritional practices that divulged from step-wise regression analysis.

6
Summary and Conclusions

Introduction

"A sound mind in a sound body" is a well known adage. A sound body is an impossibility without proper food and nourishment. The right kind of food has an important role to play in promoting good health. Healthy men have good stamina and physique, are active mentally and physically, have good endurance, have a cheerful mind and are good natured.

A majority of the world's population live in poor countries in which food is not plentiful. Most of the people in these countries either do not have enough to eat or do not have the right kind of foods. Food available for young children are particularly unsuitable.

Malnutrition is widely prevalent in India. Nearly two-thirds of India's population is on a nutritionally deficient diet. Several surveys have shown that a large number of people eat less food than they need, the worst sufferers being pregnant women. Lactating mothers and children. Malnutrition is not exclusively due to non-availability of nutritious food. Failure to use the available resources in a meaningful manner can be another cause. This is mainly due to lack of knowledge of the value of foods in relation to the needs of the individual. Ignorance and superstitions play a great role in the rejection of low-cost, locally available nutritious foods. The magnitude of malnutrition and the ignorance about the relationship of food to health among a majority of the population project the need for nutrition education and training at all levels. Nutrition education in a broad sense is a life long process, and it may bring about changes in knowledge, attitudes and practices in meeting individual and community needs. One of the programmes in vogue to provide such a knowledge to a large number of illiterates is the Adult Education Programme (AEP) wherein nutrition is incorporated in the curriculum. However, whether the instructors are properly equipped with the knowledge of nutrition, whether they possess favourable attitudes and right practices of nutrition is doubtful. Hence, the present study aimed at identifying the existing levels of knowledge, attitudes and practices of nutrition among adult education instructors so as to help develop their competence and to upgrade the technical know-how of the instructors for better instruction.

Statement of the Problem

"Knowledge, Attitudes and Practices of Nutrition Among Adult Education Programme Instructors in Andhra Pradesh".

Objectives of the Study

The main objectives of the study were :

1. to asses the levels of knowledge, attitudes and practices of nutrition among adult education programme instructors in Andhra Pradesh;
2. to suggest the probable items of nutrition that can be incorporated in the training programme course content of the adult education instructors on the basis of the gaps in knowledge, attitudes and practices;
3. to find out the influence of socio, economic and demographic factors on the knowledge, attitudes and practices of nutrition among adult education instructors;
4. to assess the inter-relationship among knowledge, attitudes and practices in nutrition of adult education instructors;
5. to study the differential contribution of the socio, economic and demographic variables in predicting the knowledge, attitudes and practices of nutrition among adult education instructors.

Hypotheses

On the basis of the above objectives, the following hypotheses were formulated.

1. The levels of knowledge, attitudes and practices of nutrition among adult education instructors are inadequate.
2. There exists variations in the level of knowledge, attitudes and practices on different items of nutrition among the adult education instructors.
3. There would not be any significant influence of socio, economic and demographic factors on the knowledge of nutrition among adult education instructors (Each one of the independent variables will be considered separately to test the hypothesis).
4. The influence of socio, economic and demographic factors on the attitude of adult education instructors towards nutrition would not be significant (Each one of the independent variables will be considered separately to test the hypothesis).
5. The practices of nutrition among adult education instructors would not be significantly influenced by their socio, economic and demographic factors (Each one of the independent variables will be considered separately to test the hypothesis).
6. There exists a positive and significant inter-relationships between the knowledge, attitudes and practices of nutrition among adult education instructors.
7. The contribution of socio, economic and demographic variables in predicting the knowledge of nutrition among adult education instructors would not vary significantly.
8. There would not be any significant variation in the amount of contribution made by different socio-economic and demographic variables to the prediction of attitudes of adult education instructors towards nutrition.
9. The contribution of socio, economic and demographic variables in predicting the practices of nutrition among adult education instructors would not vary significantly.

Variables Studied

To carry out the investigation, apart from the three dependent variables, viz., knowledge, attitudes and practices, the following independent variables were included in the study : (1) Age, (2) Sex, (3) Annual income of the family, (4) Caste (5) Religion, (6) Marital status, (7) Occupation, (8) Education status, (9) Type of the family, (10) Size of the family, (11) Experience as an adult education instructor, (12) Reading Newspapers, (13) Listening to Radio, (14) Viewing Films, (15) Viewing Filmshows and (16) Viewing Television.

Tools Used

1. To measure nutrition knowledge of instructors knowledge test was developed. All the scientific principles to be followed in the construction of a test were observed. Based on the results of pilot study conducted on 370 subjects, item analysis was carried out and item discrimination values and item difficultly values were computed for all the 63 items in pilot form of the test. Considering these two criterion 35 items were selected for the final form of the test. Face validity, content validity, item validity and intrinsic validity of the test were established. The split-half reliability of the test was 0.84.

2. To measure the nutrition attitudes of instructors an attitude scale was developed by following the Likert method of summated ratings. All the scientific principles were followed in the construction of the scale. Based on the results of pilot study conducted on 370 subjects, item analysis was done for all the 63 items in the pilot form of the scale. Considering the 't' value criteria, 35 items were selected for the final form of the scale. Face validity, content validity, item validity and intrinsic validity of the scale were established. The split-half reliability of the scale was 0.88.

3. To measure the nutritional practices of the instructors a check-list was developed. All the scientific principles required for the construction of check-list were followed. Based on the results of pilot study conducted on 370 respondents, item difficulty values and item discrimination values were computed for all the

63 items in the pilot form of the check-list. Considering the above criterion 35 items were selected for the final form of the check-list. Face validity, content validity, item validity and intrinsic validity of the check-list were established. The split-half reliability of the check-list was 0.87.

4. The data regarding personal and demographic variables were collected with the help of a personal data sheet prepared separately for the purpose.

Locale of the Study

The locale of the study was the State of Andhra Pradesh in India. The adult education programme was in operation in all the 23 districts of Andhra Pradesh during 1987–88. There were 46 projects in all the 23 districts of Andhra Pradesh.

Sample Selected

The multi-stage random sampling technique was followed in selecting the sample for the study. As the study was related to adult education programme instructors of Andhra Pradesh, the State was first stratified according to the regions, viz., Rayalaseema, Coastal Andhra (Circars) and Telengana. Two districts from each of the three regions were selected at random, viz., Chittoor and Anantapur districts from Rayalaseema, Prakasam and Krishan districts from the Circars and Khammam and Warangal districts from Telengana. After obtaining the number of projects in those six districts, one project from each of the selected districts was selected at random, thus making the total number of projects as six. In the third stage, out of 300 instructors in each project 100 were selected randomly. The Adult Education Project has 10 sectors, each sector with 30 adult education instructors in charge of a supervisor. 10 adult education instructors from each sector were selected on random basis. Thus a total of 600 adult education instructors working in the six adult education projects of six districts of three regions of Andhra Pradesh formed the final sample of the study.

Collection of Data

After establishing good rapport with the adult education instructors, the nutrition schedule was administered to them. The purpose of the study was made clear to the instructors and they were requested to respond freely. The doubts raised by them were clarified. After administering the schedule, the duly filled in schedules were collected by the investigator after checking whether all the questions were answered by the respondents. Thus the data were collected from all the 600 instructors included in the study.

Scoring and Analysis

All the tools were scored by assigning the appropriate weights to obtain numerical values on the various variables measured. The total scores obtained by each of the 600 respondents on all the variables were computed. The data were carefully analysed by employing appropriate statistical techniques like 't' test, 'F' ratio, Kramer's test, etc., to know whether the independent variables could influence significantly the dependent variables.

The correlation coefficient 'r' was computed to find out the inter-relationship between knowledge, attitudes and practices.

The simple correlation coefficient 'r' was computed between each one of the 16 independent variables and (1) knowledge, (2) attitudes and (3) practices of nutrition to identify the most significant variables associated with dependent variables, viz., knowledge, attitudes and practices. The multiple correlation coefficient 'R' was calculated by carrying out the step-wise regression analysis to find out the differential contribution of socio, economic and demographic variables in predicting the three dependent variables—knowledge, attitudes and practices.

Major Findings of the Study

1. The levels of knowledge, attitudes and practices of nutrition among adult education instructors are adequate.

2. There are variations in the level of knowledge, attitudes and practices on different items of nutrition among the adult education instructors.

3. Out of 16 socio, economic and demographic factors, 12 variables, namely, Age, Sex, Annual Income of the Family, Caste, Marital Status, Occupation, Educational Status, Family Type, Size of the Family, Experience as an Adult Education Instructor. Reading Newspapers and Listening to Radio had significantly

influenced the knowledge of nutrition among adult education instructors (Variables already discussed under Table 5.89).

4. Among the 16 socio, economic and demographic variables only 8 variables viz., Age, Annual Income of the Family, Marital Status, Occupation, Education Status, Family Type, Size of the Family and Listening to Radio influenced significantly the attitudes toward nutrition among adult education instructors (For details see Table 5.89).

5. The practices of nutrition among adult education instructors are significantly influenced by ten socio, economic and demographic variables, namely, Sex, Caste, Education Status, Family Type, Size of the Family, Experience as an Adult Education Instructor, Reading Newspapers, Listening to Radio, Viewing Filmshows and Viewing Television (For details see Table 5.89).

6. The three dependent variables viz., Knowledge, Attitudes and Practices were positively and significantly interrelated. Knowledge influenced practices both directly and indirectly as mediated by attitudes concurrently.

7. The multiple correlation between knowledge and the six significant socio, economic and demographic variables—Sex, Education, Age, Listening to Radio, Size of the Family and Experience as an Adult Education Instructor put together was 0.352. They could explain only 12.41 per cent of the variance in knowledge of nutrition. Out of this, 3.38 per cent of the variance was accounted for by Sex, 2.79 per cent by Education, 1.75 per cent by Age, 1.35 per cent by Listening to Radio, 1.62 per cent by Size of the Family and 1.52 per cent by Experience as an Adult Education Instructor. It means that there was differential contribution by these variables to the prediction of knowledge on nutrition. The remaining ten variables did not significantly contribute to the prediction of nutrition knowledge.

8. Out of 16 socio, economic and demographic variables, only five variables contributed significantly to the prediction of 'Attitudes toward Nutrition' and they were Education, Size of the Family, Age, Occupation and Annual Income of the Family. The multiple correlation between attitudes and the five independent variables was 0.2756. They could explain only 7.6 per cent of

the variance in attitudes toward nutrition. Out of this, 3.69 per cent of the variance was accounted for by Education, 1.15 per cent by Size of the Family, 1.44 per cent by Age, 0.61 per cent by Occupation and 0.71 per cent by Annual Income of the Family. It can be concluded that the extent of amount of contribution of these variables to the prediction of attitudes toward nutrition was different.

9. The six variables, namely, Education, Sex, Newspaper Reading, Type of the Family, Experience as an Adult Education Instructor and Size of the Family turned out to be significant predictors of the practices of nutrition. The multiple correlation between practices and the said six variables put together was 0.3424. The total variance explained by the six variables put together would be 11.72 per cent. Out of this, 2.89 per cent of variance was accounted for by Education, 1.84 per cent by Sex, 3.14 per cent by Newspaper Reading, 1.35 per cent by Type of the Family, 1.17 per cent by Experience as an Adult Education Instructors and 1.32 per cent by Size of the Family. It means that there was differential contribution by these variables to the prediction of practices of nutrition.

Suggestions for Further Research

1. The study of knowledge, attitudes and practices on adult learners may be attempted.
2. Since the aim of nutrition education is to adopt right practices of nutrition, factors contributing the adoption of practices of nutrition may be identified.
3. The effectiveness of strategies for launching nutrition education particularly to rural poor may be identified.
4. The nutritional education needs of rural masses may be assessed.
5. A comparative study of knowledge, attitudes and practices between elementary school teachers, non-formal education teachers and adult education organisers may be attempted.
6. Knowledge, attitudes and practices study on educationally disadvantaged women may be tried.

Bibliography

Achaya, K.T. (1974), Perspectives in Research on Food and Nutrition in India. *Proc. Nutr. Soc. India*, 16 : 22.

Adams, S.G. (1964), *Measurement and Evaluation in Education, Psychology and Guidance*, Holt, Rinehart and Winston INC., New York.

Adivi Reddy, A. (1976), *Extension Education*, Srilakshmi Press, Bapatla, Second Edition, p. 7–10.

Albanese, N.G. (1976), A Gain Step in Nutrition Education, *School Lunch Journal*, 25 : 106.

Alford, B.B. and Tibbets, M.H. (1971), Education Increases the Consumption of Vegetables by Children, *J. Nutr. Educ.*, 3:12.

Allport, G.W. (1929), The Composition of Political Attitudes. *American Journal of Sociology*, 52, 117–132.

Amala Kumari, P. (1979), Study of the Efficiency of Four Selected Approaches in Nutrition Education Given to Urban Mothers. Thesis submitted to Sri Venkateswara University, Tirupati, in partial fulfilment of the requirements for the Degree of Master of Science (Home Science) (unpublished).

Amundson, L.A. (1941), A Study of the Knowledge and Needs in Nutrition of Adult Student Home-makers, Master's thesis, Stout Institute, Madison, Wisconsin.

Anand, D., and Rao, R.A. (1962), Feeding Practices of Infants and Toddlers in Najafgarh Area. *Indian Journal of Child Health*. 11 (172).

Arora, D.D., and Kwal, K.K. (1973), Feeding Practices During the First Five Years Among Central Indian Communities, *Indian Journal of Paediatrics*. 40 (205, 208, 212, 215 & 305).

Awasthi, N.N., Anil, L.K. and Mathur, B.D. (1983), Feeding and Rearing Practices in Rural Areas of Jhansi Bandelkhad, *The Journal of Paediatrics*. 50 (902).

Baldwin, J.M. (1905), *Dictionary of Philosophy and Psychology*. Macmillan, New York.

Beker, M. (1977), A Man-made Disease. *World Health*. The Magazine of the World Health Organisation, W.H.O. p. 5.

Bell, C.G. and Lamb, M.W. (1973), Nutrition Education and Dietary Behaviour of Fifth Graders, *J. Nutr. Educ.*, 5:196–200.

Bender, A.E. (1982), *Dictionary of Nutrition and Food Technology*. p. 159.

Berg, Alan. (1973), The Nutrition Factors—Its Role in National Development, The Brookings Institution, Washington, D.C.

Bertelsen, P.H. (1974), Adult Education : A Position Paper, Unpublished Report to UNESCO, p. 4.

Beteille, A. (1971), *Caste, Class and Power*. University of California Press, Barkelay.

Bhandari, N.R. and Patel, G.P. (1973), Dietary and Feeding Habits of Infants in Various Socio-economic Groups, *Indian Journal of Paediatrics*. 10 (233).

Bhatia, R.H. (1976), *Elements of Social Psychology*. Somaya Publications Pvt. Ltd., Bombay, 3rd edition.

Bhattacharya, V. (1976), *Communication in a Gobal Village*. Chetana Publications, New Delhi.

Bloom, B.S. (1956), *Taxanomy of Education Objectives*. Vol. 1. David Mckay Company, INC. New York, 44–49.

Bogardus, E.W. (1941), *Fundamental Social Psychology*, Century,

New York, 62.

Bose, S.P. (1964), *The Diffusion of Farm Practice in Indian Villages*, R.S., 29 (1).

Briggs, G.A. (1969), The Need for Nutrition Education, *J. Nutr. Educ.*, 1:1.

Brinton, J.E. (1961), Deriving an Attitude Scale from Semantic Differential Data. *Public Opinion Quart.*, 25:289–298.

Brown, A.M., McKenzie, J.C. and Yudkin. J. (1963), Knowledge of Nutrition Amongst Housewives in London Suburbs. *Nutrition*. 17 : 16–20.

Brun, J. (Ed) (1985), The Process of Nutrition Education. A Model for Effectiveness. *J. Nutr. Educ.*, 1–21.

Burgess, E.W., Locke, H.J., and Mary, M.T. (1963), *The Family, Van Nostrand Reinhold Company*, New York, 4th Edition.

Carruth, B.R., and Force (1971), Cartoon Approach to Nutrition Education, J. Nutr. Educ., 3:57.

Carruth, B.R., and Anderson, H.L. (1977), Scaling Criteria in Developing and Evaluating and Attitude Instrument, J.Am. Dietet. Association. 70:42–46.

Carruth, B.R., Mangel, M. and Anderson, H.L. (1977), Assessing Change Proneness and Nutrition Related Behaviours. *J. Nutr. Educ.*, 70:47–52.

Cash, W.J. (1954), The Mind of the South. *Garden City*, New York, Double Day.

Census of India (Registrar General), (1981), Series 1, Paper 1.

Cerqueira, M.T. et al., (1979), A Comparison of Mass Media Techniques and a Direct Method for Nutrition Education in Rural Mexico. *J. Nutr. Educ.*, 11(2):133–137. As given in Nutrition Education in Communities of the Third World. Nestle Foundation, 1982.

Chandler, W. (1985), Teaching Mothers Saves Lives. *People*. 12:28.

Chaplin. J.P. (1975). *Dictionary of Psychology*. Dell Publishing Co. INC. New York, p. 398.

Childs, Harwood, L. (1965), *Public Opinion Nature, Formation and Role*. D Van Nostrand Company, INC. New York.

Cook, S.W. and Sellitz, C.A. (1964), A Multiple Indicator Approach to Attitude Measurement. *Psychological Bulletin*, 62:36–55.

Coleman, J.C. (1975), *Abnormal Psychology and Modern Life*. Russi J. Taraporevala for D–B, Taraporevala Sons and Co., Foruth edition, p. 762–771.

Cutting, W.A.M. (1975), The Under Fives Clinic at Block Level., *Indian Paediatric*. XII (1):123–125.

Dastur, K.S., Kundapur, S., Eswaran, S. (1977), Nutrition Education in the Community. *Proc. Nutr. Soc. India*, 21:10–16.

Datta Banik, N.D. (1977), Some Observations on Feeding Programmes, Nutrition and Growth of Pre-school Children in an Urban Community, *Indian Journal of Paediatrics*. 44(353) : 140–147.

Davidson, S., Passmore, R. and Brock, J.F. (1973), *Human Nutrition and Dietetics*. The English Language Book Society and Churchill Livingstone, Great Britain, 15th edition, p. 318.

Davey, P.L.H. and Mc Naughton, J.M. (1969), Nutrition in Developing Countries, *Nutr. Newsletter*, F.A.O., 7:34:36.

Devadas, R.P. and Easwaran, P. (1967), Influence of Socio-Economic Factors on the Nutritional Status and Food Intake of Pre-school Children in a Rural Community. *J. Nutr. Dietet*. 4:156–161.

Devadas, R.P. (1968), Social and Cultural Factors Influencing Malnutrition. *Proc. Nutr. Soc. India.*, 6:22.

Devadas, R.P., Chandrasekhar, U. (1970), Nutrition Education of Illiterate People. *J. Nutr. Educ*. 1:13–16.

Devadas, R.P., (1972), Nutrition in Tamil Nadu. Sangam Publishers, Madras 600 001.

Devadas, R.P. Chandrasekhar, U. and Yesodha, T. (1974), Scope for Nutrition Education in the Primary School Lunch Programme Through the Curriculum. *Indian J. Nutr. Diet*. 111:321–337.

Devadas, R.P. (1974), Social and Economic Dimensions of Nutrition. *Proc. Nutr. Soc. India*. 17:66–72.

Devadas, R.P., Jayapoorani, N., Gowri, T.S. (1977), The Nutritional Knowledge and Practices of the Rural Home Makers in a Post and Non-ANP Block. *Ind. J. Nutr. Dietet.* 14:157–160.

Devadas, R.P. (1977), Need for Nutrition Education, *Proc. Nutr. Soc. Ind.* 21:1–9.

Devadas, R.P. (1979), Nutrition and Dietary Needs of Infants and Children. Symposium on Food Needs of Infants and Children. *Organisation of Food Scientists and Technologists.* India, p. 15.

Devadas, R.P. (1980), Nutrition and Health Education. *Proc. Nutr. Soc.* Ind. 25:61–66.

Devadas, R.P.; Leelavathy, K.C. and Jacob, A. (1982), Initiating Activities for Rural Women's Clubs in Coimbatore District. *Indian J. Nutr. Diet.*, 19:252-254.

Devadas, R.P., Sitalakshmi,S. and Padmakumari, S. (1982) Nutrition Education Programme inNaicken Palayam Village. *Indian J. Nutr. Diet.*, 19:258-259.

Devadas, R.P., Sitalakshmi, S. and Vijayambal, C. (1982) Improving the Health, Nutrition and Sanitary Conditions in Villages Through the Education of Women and Children. *Indian J. Nutr. Diet.*, 19:255-257.

Devadas, R.P. (1986), Nutrition Education in India — Impact on Knowledge, Behaviour and Health Status of Students. *J. Nutr. Educ.*, 18:111–115.

Dugdale, A.E., Chandler, D. and Baghurst, K. Knowledge and Belief in Nutrition. *Amer. J. Clin. Nutr.*, 32:441-445.

Edwards, A.L. (1957), Techniques of Attitude Scale Construction, Appleton Century Craft, INC. New York, p. 153.

Edwards, A.L. and Kilpatrick (1948), Quoted from Edward, A.L. (1957) Scale Analysis and the Measurement of Social Attitudes. *Ibid.*

Edwards, A.L. (1969), *Techniques of Attitude Scale Construction.* Vakils Feffer and Simmons Private Ltd., Bombay, p.2, 13-14, 152.

Emmons, L., Hayes, M. (1973), Nutrition Knowledge of Mothers and

Children. *J. Nutr. Educ.*, 5:134.

Eppright (1966), E.S. Tests of Nutrition Knowledge and Attitudes. Iowa Agric. and Home Econ. *Expert. Sta. Project* No. 665–H.

Eppright E.S., Fox, B.A., Fryer, G.H., Lamkin Vivian, V.M. (1970), The North Central Regional Study of Diets of Pre-school Chidlren. 2-Nutrition Knowledge and Attitudes of Mothers. *J. Home. Econ.*, 62:327.

Ferry, B. (1981), *Breast Feeding : Comparative Studies, Cross National Summaries*, World Fertility Survey, International Statistics Institute, 13.

Fishbein, M. and Ajzen, I. (1975), *Belief Attitude, Intention and Behaviour*. Addison Wesley Reading. 56-60.

Fleigal, F.C. (1957), *Farm Income and the Adoption of Farm Practices*, R.S. 22 (2).

Frank, C. (1967), *Stratificaiton and Risk Taking — A Theory Tested on Agricultural Innovation*, A.S.R. 32(2).

Freedman, J.L., Carlsmith, J.M. and Sears, D.O. *Social Psychology* (1974), Prentice Hall, Englewood Cliffs, N.J. 50–55.

Freeman, F.S. (1967), *Theory and Practice of Psychological Testing*, Oxford and IBH Publishing Co., New Delhi, 108–116.

Garrett, H.E. and Wood Worth, R.S. (1979), *Statistics in Psychology and Education*, 9th Indian Reprint, Vakils Feffer and Simons Ltd., Bombay.

Ghai, O.P., Jaiswal, V.N. and Seth, V. (1971), Infantile Diarrhoea in Relation to Feeding Practices, *Indian Journal of Paediatric*, 38:354.

Ghosh, Shanti (1977), *Feeding and Care of Infants and Young Children*. Voluntary Health Association of India, New Delhi.

Ghosh, S., Gidwani, S., Mittal, S.K. and Verma, R.K. (1976), Sociocultural Factors Affecting Breast Feeding and Mother Infant Feeding Practices in an Urban Community. *Indian Journal of Paediatrics.*, 13(826) : 827.

Gillespe, A.H. (1981), Applying Communication Theory in Nutrition Education Research. *J. Nutr. Educ.*, Supplement. 13(1) : 29–33.

Glanz, K. (1981), Social Psychological Perspectives and Applications to Nutrition Education. *J. Nutr. Educ.*, 13:66-69.

Gopalan, C. (1966), Major Nutritional Problems of India and South East Asia. Proc. Seventh. Int. *Congress of Nutr.*, Hamburg, III. p. 320.

Gopalan, C. (1973), *The Terrible Ravages of Malnutrition.* The UNESCO Courier, 28:24.

Gopalan, C. (1977), Nutrition and National Development. *Proc. Nutr. Soc. India.* 21:29-31.

Gould, M.A. (1963), The Adaptive Functions of Castes in Contemporary Indian Society. *Asian Survey.* 3.

Greaves, J.P. (1975), Nutrition Education or Education in Child Care. *J. Trop. Paed.*, 21:293-294.

Gronlund, N.E. (1968), *Constructing Achievement Tests.* Prentice-Hall INC., Englewood Cliffs, N.J. p. 86-87.

Gronlund, N.E. (1970), Stating Behavioural Objectives for Class Room Instruction. The Macmillan Company, 866, Third Avenue, New York, 10022, Collier, Fourth Printing, p. 18--19.

Guilford, J.P. (1954), *Psychometric Methods.* 2nd Ed. Tara McGraw Hill Publishing Company, Faridabad, Haryana, p. 399.

Gupta, A.A. and Singh, K. (1981), Health Awareness Among Adolescents as a Dependent Function of Age, Family Income and Size, *Indian Education Review*, NCERT, New Delhi, 16:4.

Gupta, V., Misra, V.L., Rathi, A.K. and Srivasthava, J.R. (1979), Adolescents and Knowledge of Population Dynamics and Family Planning. *The Indian Journal of Family Welfare*, 25(3) : 235.

Guthrie, G.M. (1981), *Prizes for Prudent Mothers.* Development Forum, 9(3):6-7.

Higgins, M., Montague, J. (1972), Nutrition Education Through Mass Media in Korea. *J. Nutr. Educ.*, 4(2):58-62.

Hochbaum, G.M. (1979), *Nutrition Behaviour and Education in Nutrition Lipids and Coronary Heart Diseases.* R. Kevy et al., eds. Ravem Press, New York. 365-368.

Hochbaum, G.M. (1980), Patient Counselling Vs Patient Teaching. *Clinical Nursing*, 2:1–8.

Hachbaum, G.M. (1981), Strategies and Their Rationale for Changing People's Eating Habits. *J. Nutr. Educ.*, 13:59–65.

Hogarth, R. (Ed) (1981), Question Framing and Response Consistency. San Francisco Jossay-Bass. 20–25.

Hoorweg, J.C. and McDowell, I. (1979), Evaluation of Nutrition Education in Africa Community Research in Uganda, 1971-72. Mouton Publishers. The Netherlands. 158-160.

Hornby, A.S., Cowie, A.P., and Lewis, J.W. (1968), *Oxford Advanced Learner's Dictionary of Current English.* The English Language Book Society, Oxford University Press, London.

ICMR Studies on Pre-school Children (1977). Report on the Working Party of Indian Council of Medical Research. *Tech. Rep. Series* No. 26.

ICMR (1985) Preliminary Report of a Collaborative Study on Identification of High Risk Families, Mothers and Their Offspring With Particular Reference to the Problem of Maternal Nutrition, Low Birth Weight, Perinatal and Infant Mortality, Morbidity in Rural and Urban Slum Mothers. *ICMR*. UNICEF. Assisted Study (Mimeograph).

Insko, C. and Schopler, J. (1967), Triadic Consistency : A Statement of Affective-Cognitive Connotative Consistency. *Psychological Review.*, 74:361–376.

Ismail, J.A., Kanawati, A.A., McLaren, D.S. (1975), Formal Education of Mothers and Their Nutrition Behaviour. *J. Nutr. Educ.*, 7(1):22.

Jalso, S.B., Burns, M.M., Rivers, J.M. (1965), Nutritional Beliefs and Practices in Relation to Demographic and Personal Characteristics. *J. Amer. Diet. Ass.*, 47:263–266.

Jelliffe, D.B. (1968), *Infant Nutrition in the Sub-tropics.* WHO Monograph Series No. 29, 2nd Ed. WHO : Geneva.

John Hopkins University School of Hygiene and Public Health (1976), The Functional Analysis of Health Needs and Services, Asia Publishing House, Bombay.

Kahneman, D. and Tversky, A. (1979), Prospect Theory : An Analysis of Decision Under Risk. *Econometrica*, 47:263–291.

Kamala Gopala Rao (1983), Fertility Control as a Strategy to Ensure Proper Nutrition for Women by 2000 A.D. Paper Presented during the Seminar on Nutrition and Development—Focus on Women at Lady Irwin Colleg, New Delhi.

Kelly, S.G. (1977), *Principles of Social Psychology*. Winthrop Publishers INC. Cambridge, 167–70, 199–205.

King, D.W. (1977), *Food, Agriculture & Nutrition*. p. 378.

Kivlin Joseph, E., Fleigel Frederick, C., Roy, P., and Sen, K.L. (1971), Innovations in Rural India, Browling Green State University Press, USA.

Kohler, W. (1929), *Gestalt Psychology*. Liveright, New York.

Kolasa, K., Wenger, A., Paolucci, B., and Bobbitt, N. (1979), Home Based Learning—Implications for Nutrition Educators. *J. Nutr. Educ.*, 11:19–21.

Kolasa, K.M. (1981), Nutritional Anthropologists and Nutrition Educators—Potentials for a Multi-dimensional World Review, *J. Nutr. Educ.*, 17:9–11.

Kothari, C.R. (1986), *Research Methodology—Methods and Techniques*, Wiley Eastern Limited, New Delhi.

Kramer, C.Y. (1956), Extension of Multiple Range Tess to Group Means with Unequal Numbers of Replications. *Biometrics*, Sep. p. 307–310.

Krause, O.T. and Fox, M.H. (1977), Nutrition Knowledge and Attitudes of Physicians. *J. Am. Dietet. Assoc.*, 70:607.

Krech and Crutchfield (1948), *Theory and Problems of Social Psychology*, McGraw-Hill Co., London, p. 219.

Kusuma, D.L. (1987), Receiptivity to Nutrition Education Among a Select Group of Rural Women. An unpublished Theis submitted to S.V. University, Tirupati in fulfilment of M.Phil. Degree.

Leverton, M.R. (1974), What is Nutrition Education ? *J. Am. Dietetc.* Assoc. 64 : 17.

Lewin, K. (1943), Forces Behind Food Habits and Methods of Change. In the Problem of Changing Food Habits, *Nutr. Res. Counc. Bulletin.*, 108:35–36.

Lindquist, E.F. (1966), Educational Measurement, Washington D.C. *American Council on Education*, p. 672.

Liska, A. (Ed.) (1975), *The Consistency Controversy : Readings on the Impact of Attitude on Behaviour.* New York, John Wiley, 99–109.

Liveright and Haygood, N. (Eds) (1967), The Exerter Papers. Boston, p. 9.

Lovett, R., Baker, E., Marcus, B. (1970), The Effect of a Nutrition Education Programme at the Second Grade Level. *J. Nutr. Educ.*, 2:80.

Lowenberg, M.E., Todhunter, N., Wilson, E.E., Freeny, M.C., Savage, J.R. (1970), *Food and Man.* Wiley Eastern Privaté Ltd., New Delhi, First Edition, 97.

Madhavi, V., Rao, N.D., and Mathur, Y.C. (1973), Feeding and Weaning Practices in the Village Fatehpur-Hyderabad, *Indian Journal of Paediatrics*, 9, (480).

Magnus Pyke (1958), *Nutrition.* The English Universities Press Ltd. 102, Newgate Street, London, RCI, p. 6.

Majumdar, A.K., and Das, K.K. (1972), Some Aspects of Adoption of Family Planning Practices in Indian Villages. *The Journal of Family Welfare*, 28(3).

Malinowski, B. (1961), Argonauts of the Western Pacific, Dutton and Co., New York. 7.

Manocha, S.L. (1972), *Malnutrition and Retarded Human Development.* Charles C. Thomas Publishers. Springfield. Illinois, U.S.A., p. 340–346.

Manoff, R.K. (1980), The Effective Use of Mass Media in Nutrition Education. *PAG Bull.*, 4(1) : 12–17.

Mannoni, O.P., and Caliban (1964), *The Psychology of Colonization*, New York. Praeger.

Meclintock, G.C. (1972), Experimental Social Psychology, Holt Rinehart and Winston, *INC*. New York, 108–140.

McClosky, G. (1967), *Education and Public Understanding*. Harper and Row.

McDowell, E.E. (1975), The Semantic Differential as a Method of Teacher Evaluation. *J. Ed. Res.*, 68:330–333.

McDougall, G. Claxton, J., Ritchie, J and Anderson, C. (1981), Consumer Energy Research : A Review. *Con. Res.*, 8:343–354.

McNutt, K.W. (1977), Public Understanding of Nutrition Implications for Educational Programmes. *Contemporary Nutrition*, 2:1–2.

Mead, M. (1962), Culture Change in Relation to Nutrition—Malnutrition and Food Habits. Report of an International and Inter-Professional Conference. Edited by Anne Burgess and Dean R.F.A. Tavistock Publications. The World Foundation for Mental Health, p. 50–61.

Mehta, T.S. (1972), *Population Education*, NCERT, New Delhi.

Menon, A.G.G., Prema, L. (1977), Attitudes of Village Women Towards Training in Applied Nutrition. *Indian J. Adult Educ.*, 38, 8/9:32–39.

Morgan, J.J.B. (1934), *Keeping a Sound Mind*. Macmillan & Co., New York.

Mosley, H.W., Werner, L.H., and Becker, S. (1982), The Dynamics of Birth Spacing and Marital Fertility in Kenya, *World Fertility Survey*, ISI, 30.

Mukherjee, P.S. (1969), Feeding of Children in Urban West Bengal, Calcutta, *Indian Journal of Paediatrics*. 26(467).

Munoz De Chavez, M. (1972), Improving Nutrition in the Less Developed Areas, *J. Nutr. Educ.*, 4:167–170.

Muthayya, B.C. (1972), *Child Welfare*, National Institute of Community Development, Hyderabad.

Muthayya, B.C. (1974), Attitudes of Rural Parents Toward Certain Aspects of Child Rearing Practices, *Indian Educational Review*, 9:48.

Murthy, M.S.R. (1981), Adult As a Learner—Paedogogical Perspectives. *Quest in Education.* 18(2).

Nagwekar, A. (1972), Educational Needs of Rural Mothers of Children Under Five Years of Age in Selected Nine Aspects of Child Nutrition. A Thesis submitted to M.S. University, Baroda.

Naidu, J.S. (1981), Communication and Education Strategy for Rural Development With Special Reference to Population Education for Out of School Youth, M.Phil Dissertation, S.V. University, Tirupati.

Nancy Raper (1970), Pocket Dictionary. Churchill Livingstone. British Commonwealth Nurses War Memorial Fund Research Fellow. 13th edition.

Narayana, I.P., Dhanabalan, M., Rao, D.C.V., Fernandez, A., and Balakrishna, S. (1974), Some Infant Feeding and Rearing Practices in a Rural Community in Pondichery, *Indian Journal of Paediatrics.* 11(667).

NIN Ann. Rep. (1976-1978, 1980-82), National Institute of Nutrition, Hyderabad, India.

NNMB Surveys (1976, 1977, 1980), National Institute of Nutrition, Hyderabad, India.

Nisbett, R. and Ross, L. (1980), *Human Inference Strategies and Shortcoming of Social Judgement*, Englewood Cliffs, NJ : Prentice Hall, 104–120.

Nunnally, J.C. (1959), *Test and Measurement*, McGraw-Hill Book Co., New York, p. 305.

Obert, C.G. (1978), *Community Nutrition*, John Wiley and Sons, INC, p. 249-250.

O'Connel, L., Shannon, B. and Sims, L. (1981), Assessing Nutrition Related Attitudes and Beliefs of Teachers. *J. Nutr. Educ.*, 13:84–85.

Olson, J.C. and Sims, L.S. (1980), Assessing Nutrition Knowledge from an Information Processing Perspectives, *J. Nutr. Educ.*, 12:157.

Parvathi Rao, K. (1968), Socio-Cultural Factors and Malnutrition in

Telengana Region and Andhra Pradesh. *Proc. Nutr. Soc. India*, 6:38.

Pavalkar, Madhoo and Kulkarni, R.R. (1978), *Second Indian Studies Communications*. Popular Prakasam, Bombay.

Pelto, P.J. and Pelto, G.H. (1978), *Anthropological Research*. The Structure of Inquiry. Cambridge University Press, New York, 71-73.

Pelto, G.H. (1981), Anthropological Contributions to Nutrition Education Research. *J. Nutr. Educ.,* 13:2-8.

Perkins, L.L., Roach, P.R. and Vaden, A.G. (1980), Influence of Teachers Attitudes Toward the School Lunch Programme on Student Participation. *J. Nutr. Educ.*, 12:55-80.

Perry, R.W. (1976), Attitude Scales on Behaviour Estimation Devices : Scale Specificity and Prediction Accuracy. *The Journal of Social Psychology*, 100:137.

Peterson, M.E. and Kies, G. (1972), Nutrition Knowledge and Attitudes of Early Elementary Teachers. *J. Nutr. Educ.*, 4:11-15.

Phillips, D.E., Mary Ann Bass, Yetley, E. (1978), Use of Food Nutrition Knowledge by Mothers of Pre-school Children. J. *Nutr. Educ.*, 10(2) : 73-75.

Radolph, L.I. (1967), *The Modernity of Traditions*. Chicago University Press, Chicago.

Rajagopalan, S. (1977), Nutrition Education—Role of Voluntary Agencies. *Proc. Nutr. Soc. Ind.*, 21:17-19.

Raju, B.V., Rao, K.C. (1977), Thiru Gnanasambandam, Sundaravalli, N. Nutrition Counselling in Hospitals and Primary Health Centres. *Proc. Nutr. Soc. India*. 21:20–23.

Rajyalakshmi, P., Reddy, N.B. and Reddy, U. A Guttman (1980), Scale to Measure the Attitude of Rural Women Towards Nutrition. Maha. *Jour. of Extn. Educ.*, 11:31-38.

Ramdas Murthy (1982), What Ails Our Nutrition Education Efforts? *Nutrition News*, NIN. Hyderabad, 3(2):1-2.

Ranganathan, K.V. (1968), Some Thoughts on Nutrition Education, *Proc. Nutr. Soc. of India*, 6:1.

Rani, U.D. (1982), Cost of Rearing Children and Other Socio-Economic Determinants of Fertility. Ph.D. Thesis, S.V. University, Tirupati, p. 125.

Rao, P.T. (1957), Customs of Infants Feeding in South India, *Indian Journal of Child Health*, 7(347).

Reddy, P.R. and Chandralekha, K. (1978), Can We Use Novel Approaches Effectively ? A paper presented at Diamond Jubilee Celebrations, National Institute of Nutrition, Hyderabad.

Rhodo Ellis (1956), *Dictionary of Dietetics*, p. 202.

Ritchie, J.A.S. (1969), Learning Better Nutrition. A Second Study of Approaches and Techniques, Rome, Food and Agriculture Organisation of the United Nations, 240.

Ritchie, J., McDougall, G. and Claxton, J. (1981), Complexities to Household Energy Consumption and Conservation. *J. Con. Res.* 8:233–242.

Robinson, C.H. (1972), *Normal and Theraupeutic Nutrition*. 14th Edn. IBH Publishing Co., New Delhi, 361–375.

Roy, P., and Kivlin, J. (1968), Health Innovations and Family Planing : A Study in Eight Indian Villages, National Institute of Community Development, Hyderabad.

Roy, P. (1971), Agricultural Innovations Among Indian Farmers (in) Innovations in Rural India. Bowling Green State University Press.

Roy and Kapur, J.M. (1975), The Retention of Literacy. The Macmillan Co. of India Ltd., Delhi.

Saxena, Sand Ghai, O.P. (1968), A Study of Methods Used for Child Rearing in Bikaner. *Indian Journal of Paediatrics*, 35(342).

Schaefer, E.S. and Bell, R.Q. (1958), Development of a Parental Attitude Research Instrument. *Child Dev.*, 29:339-342.

Schwartz, N.E. (1975), Nutritional Knowledge, Attitudes and Practices of High School Graduates, *J. Am. Dietet. Assoc.*, 66:28.

Scrimshaw, N.S. (1969), Nature of Protein Requirements—Ways They Can be Met in Tommorrow's World, *J. Am. Dietet. Assoc.* 54:94–102.

Seth, V., and Ghai, O.P. (1970), Feeding Habits of Infants and Pre-school Children in Urban, Semi-urban and Rural communities. *Indian Journal of Paediatrics*, 8(452).

Sharma, A., Dharam, B., and Lahore, U.C. (1977), Knowledge and Practices of Mothers Towards Polio Drops. *Indian Journal of Paediatrics*, 44(348).

Sharma, V., Sharma, R., and Purohit, B.K. (1977), A Study of Feeding and Weaning Patterns of Sindhi Children Below 5 years in an Urban Area. *Indian Journal of Paediatrics*, 44(352) p. 166–167.

Shah, P.M. (1978), Nutrition Education Through Domiciliary Management of Energy Protein Malnutrition. *Ind. J. Nutr. Dietet.* 15:228–232.

Shanti Chakravarthy (1977), Training of Village Level Workers in Nutrition. *Proc. Nutr. Soc. India.* 21:24-26.

Shaw, M.E. and Wright, J.M. (1967), *Scales for the Measurement of Attitudes*. McGraw Hill, New York. 1-32.

Shukla, A.N. (1972), The Concept of Extensioin Education : A Study in Psycho-Physical Methods (in P.R.R. Sinha (Ed) Studies in Extension Education, National Institute of Community Development, Hyderabad, p. 17.

Sims, S.L. (1976), Demographic and Attitudinal Correlates of Nutritional Knowledge. *J. Nutr. Educ.,* 8:122.

Sims, L.S. (1981), Further Thoughts on Research Perspectives in Nutrition Education. *J. Nutr. Educ.*, 13:70-75.

Smith, L. (1963), *Killers of Dream*. Garden City. New York. Double Day.

Smith, A.L., Branch, G., Henry, S.E., Nagpuri, P.R. (1986), Effectiveness of Nutrition Education Programmes for Mothers and Their Children Under 5 Years of Age. *J. Am. Dietet. Assoc.,* 85(8).

Someswara Rao, K., Swaminathan, M.C., Swarup, S. and Patwardhan, V.N. (1959), WHO Bulletin, 20(603).

Srinivasa, M.N. (1962), *Caste in Modern India and Other Essays*. Asia Publishing House, New York.

Srinivasa, M.N. (1965), Social Change in Modern India, Berkelay University of California Press, California.

Stanfield J.P. (1976), Nutrition Education in the Context of Early Childhood Malnutrition in Low-resource Communities. *Proc. Nutr. Soc.*, 35, 131-138.

Storrer, J. (1977), Hot and Cold Food Beliefs in an Indian Community and Their Significance. *Journal of Human Nutrition.* 31:33-40.

Sudha Rani, K. (1987), An Enquiry into Nutritional Knowledge of Adult Education Programme Organisers of Puttur Block in Chittoor District. An unpublished thesis submitted to S.V. University, Tirupati for partial fulfilment of Masters Degree.

Sujatha, A.M. (1981), A Study of the Influence of Certain Selected Factors on the Nutritional Practices of Rural Mothers of the Village, S.V. University, Tirupati.

Summers, G.F. (1970), *Attitude Measurement*, Chicago. Rand McNally and Co., 50-56.

Sutnick, M.R. (1981), The 'Q' Sort Technique Applied to Nutrition Attitudes of Investigation. *J. Nutr. Edc.,* 13:102-105.

Swamy, S.B., Rao, M.K.S., Awastigar, M.B. (1978), Impact of Television on Farmers' Knowledge, *Indian Journal of Adult Education.* 39(1).

Swanson, J. (1972), Second Thoughts on Knowledge and Attitude Effects Upon Behaviour. *Journal of Social Health.* 42:363-365.

Swarnalatha, A.M. (1978), Evaluation of Four Teaching Approaches in Nutrition Education to Rural Mothers of Chandragiri Taluk. Thesis submitted to Sri Venkateswara University, Tirupati in partial fulfilment of Master's Degree.

Thaman, O.P., Anand, M.L. and Menhas, R.S. (1964), Feeding Practices of Infants and Children in Kashmir. *Indian Journal of Paediatrics.* 1(196).

Thaman, O.P. and Manchanda, S.S. (1968), Child Rearing Practices in Punjab. *Indian Journal of Paediatrics.* 35(334).

The American Dietetic Association (1973), Position, Paper on Nutrition Education. *J. Am. Dietet. Associ.*, 62:429.

The Colombia Fertility Survey, 1976 (1976) : *Summary of Findings, World Fertility Survey (WES),* International Statistical Institute (ISI), Voorburg, The Hague Netherlands.

The Haiti Fertility Survey, 1977 (1981) : *A Summary of Findings,* W.F.S., ISI, No. 31.

The Jordon Fertility Survey, 1976 (1980) : *A Summary of Findings,* W.F.S., ISI, No. 20.

The Kenya Fertility Survey, 1978 (1978) : *A Summary of Findings,* W.F.S., ISI, No. 26.

The Korean National Fertility Survey, 1974 (1974) : *A Summary of Findings,* W.F.S., ISI.

The Malaysian Fertility Survey and Family Survey (1978) : *A Summary of Findings,* W.F.S., ISI.

The Pakistan Fertility Survey (1975) : *A Summary of Findings,* W.F.S., ISI, No. 17.

The Peru Fertility Survey, 1977 (1980) : *A Summary of Findings,* W.F.S., ISI, No. 21.

The Sudan Fertility Survey, 1979 (1982) : *A Summary of Findings,* W.F.S., ISI, No. 36.

The Sri Lanka Fertility Survey, 1975 (1975) : *A Summary of Findings,* W.F.S., ISI.

Thorndike, E.L., et al. (1928), *Adult Learning*, New York, Macmillan.

Thurstone, L. (1947), *Thurstone Interest Schedule*, New York, Psychological Corp.

Tomar, B.S. and Srivastava, D.K. (1980), Family Size, Protein Intake and Malnutrition in an Industrial Area of Gwalior. *Indian Journal of Paediatrics*, 47 (386). p. 218.

Tversky, A. and Kahneman, D. (1974), Judgement Under Uncertainity : Heuristics and Biases. Science. 185:1124-1131.

Usha Devi, R. (1983), An Enquiry into Nutritional Knowledge of National Adult Education Programme Organisers of Pichatur Block of Chittoor District. An unpublished thesis submitted in partial fulfilment of Master's Degree, S.V. University, Tirupati.

Vasantha Kumari, K. (1979), A Study of the Relationship Between Nutritional Knowledge and Practices of Rural Mothers to that of the Deitary Quality and Nutritional Status of Their Children. A dissertation submitted to the Department of Home Science, S.V. University, Tirupati (unpublished).

Venkatachalam, P.S. and Rebello, I.M. (1971), Nutrition for Mother and Child. *ICMR Special Reference Serial No. 4.*

Venkatachalam, C.V., and Kulandaivel, K. (1965), A Study of the Health Concepts and Health Habits of Pupils in Some Secondary Schools in Coimbatore. *Journal of Educational Research and Extension*, 1(3) : 30-31.

Vijayadurgamba, E., Geervani, P. (1974), Diet and Nutritional Status of the Pre-school Children and Nutritional Awareness of the Mothers of Urban Slums of Hyderabad. *Ind. J. Paedia.* 46:8.

Walia, B.N.S., Ghambhai, S.K. and Bhatia, U. (1974), Breast Feeding and Weaning Practice in an Urban Population. *Indian Journal of Paediatrics*, 11(133).

Warren, H.C. (1934), *Dictionary of Psychology*, Niffillin Co., Houghton, Boston.

Watson, G. and Johnson, D.W. (1972), *Social Psychology*. Issues and Insights. Philadelphia, Lippincott, 110-140.

Webster (1975), *New World Dictionary*, Oxford and IBH Publishing Co., New Delhi, p. 88.

White, P.L. (1976), Why All he Fuss Over Nutrition Education ? *J. Nutr. Educ.*, 8(2) : 54-62.

Whitehead, F.E. (1973), Nutrition Education Research World. Rev. *Nutr. Diet.* 17:91-93 and 114-135.

Wicker, A.W. (1969), Attitude Versus Actions. The Relationship of Verbal and Overt Behavioural Responses to Attitude Objects, *J. Soc.* Issues., 25:41.

Wilder, F. (1973), Information, Education and Communication for Population and Family Planning Community and Family Study Centre, University of Chicago.

William, S.R. (1969, 1974), Nutrition and Diet Therapy. St. Louis

Mosley, London.

Wilson, J. (1976), *Indian Caste*, Deep Publications, New Delhi.

Winter (1970), Hunger and Malnutritioin. Editorial. *J. Nutr. Educ.*, 1(3):4.

Yadav, M.S., Govinda, R. (1975), Research Task in Instructional Technology. *Indian Educational Review*, 10(1).

Yankelovich, Skelly anu White (1978), INC. Nutrition : A Study of Consumer's Attitudes and Behaviour. A National Probability Study conducted for Women's Day.

Young, C.M. Waldner, B.G., Berriesford, K.W. (1956), What is the Home Maker Knows About Nutrition ? III—Relation of Knowledge to Practice. *J. Am. Dietet. Assoc.* 32:321.

Index